All-

Strangest Creatures

of the World

George Kensinger

A Ridge Press Book

Bantam Books

Toronto • New York • London

Photo Credits

A = Ardea BC = Bruce Coleman SL = Sea Library

Ron Austing (BC): 97; Jen & Des Bartlett (BC): 15 (ctr), 27, 37 (top), 45 (top left), 56, 57 (top), 58, 103, 137, 139, 153, 156; M. J. Baum (BC): 59; S. C. Bisserot (BC): 10, 11, 62, 64, 105, 112; Alan Blank (BC): 9 (btm), 16, 32, 55 (top), 90; J. R. Brownlie (BC): 12; Jane Burton (BC): 6, 9 (top left), 69, 71, 77, 99, 108, 138, 148; J. H. Carmichael, Jr. (BC): 76; Bruce Coleman: 29 (left), 33, 34, 40 (left & right), 48 (right), 49, 50 (btm right), 60, 68, 85, 93, 94, 118, 121, 127; F. Collet (A): 123; Thase Daniel: 29 (right), 83; E. R. Degginger (BC): 65; T. A. DeRoy (BC): 120 (btm); N. Devore III (BC): 114; L. R. Ditto (BC): 46 (left); Robert L. Dunne (BC): 37 (btm right), 63; E. Duscher (BC): 54; M. D. England (A): 50 (top); Francisco Erize (BC): 15 (top), 35, 38, 82; Douglas Faulkner: 102, 136, 140, 151, 154; Jean-Paul Ferrero (A): 125; Kenneth W. Fink (A): 130 (left), (BC): 81 (ctr), 109, 124, 126, 130 (right); R. L. Fleming (BC): 25; Neville Fox-Davies (BC): 132; B. Franklin (BC): 84; M. Freeman (BC): 91; Carl Gans: 131; C. Gilbert (SL): 128; Daniel W. Gotshall (SL): 143; J. C. Hookelheim (SL): 98, 104, 106 (top left & right), 111, 113, 141, 142; Eric Hosking (BC): 9 (top right), 106 (btm); D. Hughes (BC): 18, 23, 92; Marilyn K. Krog: 39, 45 (top right), 117; Frank W. Lane (BC): 57 (btm); C. Laubscher (BC): 26; J. McDonald (BC): 67; J. Markham (BC): 81 (top); F. Merlet (BC): 81 (btm); W. T. Miller (BC): 46 (right); Pat Morris (A): 9 (ctr), 101; N. Myers (BC): 116; M. Timothy O'Keefe (BC): 145, 147; David Overcash (BC): 31, 86; Oxford Scientific Films (BC): 15 (btm right), 41; R. R. Pawlowski (BC): 119; R. E. Pelham (BC): 15 (btm left), 37 (btm left); Graham Pizzey (BC): 129; G. D. Plage (BC): 78; Allan Power (BC): 135 (btm), 150, 155; H. Reinhard (BC): 21, 42, 45 (btm), 66, 73 (right), 96; Laura Riley (BC): 149; L. L. Rue III (BC): 45 (ctr), 47, 48 (left), 73 (left); G. B. Schaller (BC): 24, 75; J. R. Simon (BC): 55 (btm); Alex Smart (SL): 88; M. F. Soper (BC): 135 (top left); L. M. Stone (BC): 95; David Sumner (Amwest): 135 (top right); Simon Trevor (BC): 30, 50 (btm left); Joe Van Wormer (BC): 52, 110; J. Wallis (BC): 120 (top); Peter Ward (BC): 22.

Front Cover: Frilled lizard, J. Wallis (BC)
Back Cover: Cassowary, G. D. Dodge & D. R. Thompson (BC)
Title Page: Upside-down catfish, Douglas Faulkner

STRANGEST CREATURES OF THE WORLD
A Bantam Book published by arrangement with The Ridge Press, Inc.
Designed and produced by The Ridge Press, Inc.
For information address: The Ridge Press, Inc.,
25 West 43rd Street, New York, N.Y. 10036.
Library of Congress Catalog Card Number: 77-73672
ISBN: 0-553-11141-8
Published simultaneously in the United States and Canada.

Bantam Books are published by Bantam Books, Inc.
Its trademark, consisting of the words "Bantam Books" and the
portrayal of a bantam, is registered in the United States Patent Office
and in other countries. Marca Registrada.
Bantam Books, Inc., 666 Fifth Avenue, New York, N.Y. 10019
Printed in Italy by Mondadori Editore, Verona.

Contents

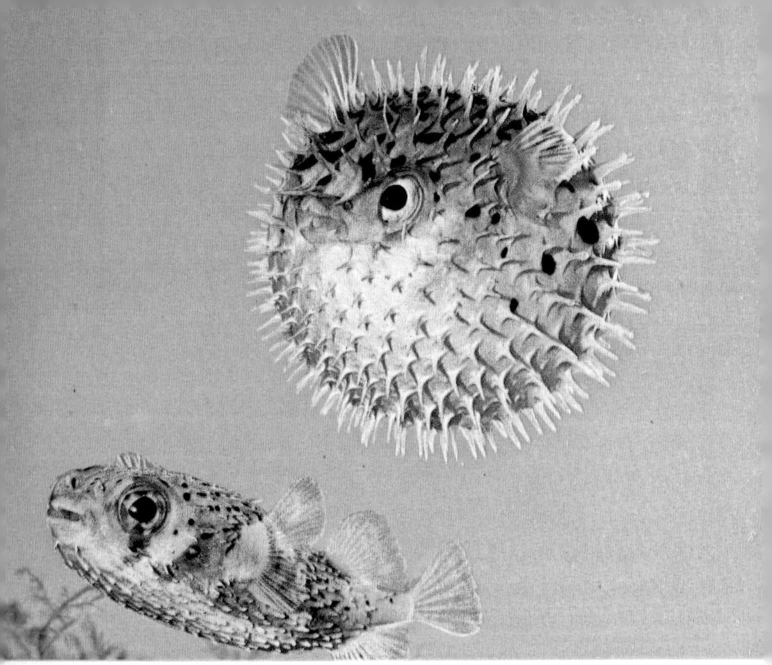

Introduction

Among natures's creatures, totaling more than a million species, are examples of incredible beauty, grace, and performance, living jewels and unbelievably complex perfections of organic engineering. Other animals appear freakish, at least to human eyes. Most of these are cases where function has taken precedence over appearance, resulting in animals that appear odd or even ugly though they may achieve with great success the biological goals of all species: survival and procreation. In some instances both beauty and function have been lost through evolution, and the animal's appearance has no rational explanation in terms of need. In some respects the reasons for including some of the animals in this book follow an equally unexplainable pattern. You will find some animals that are beautiful, exotic, and rare, others that are common but have unusual habits or features. Depending on how the word

▲ Puffers, normal (left) and inflated

is defined, almost all animals are "strange" at least to some degree, for each has its peculiarity of structure or habits that equip it for a particular way of life. With such a broad definition, oddities in nature are indeed the rule rather than the exception.

This book highlights some of the strange creatures among animals with backbones, or vertebrates: the fishes, amphibians, reptiles, birds, and mammals. Excluded is that vast world of animals without backbones, the invertebrates, representing more than 90 percent of all animals in number of species. Excluded also, though perhaps in many ways the strangest creature of all, is man, who is structurally rather ordinary and lacking a uniqueness of specialization that marks many others. But with the one distinctive feature that has set him apart—his ability to think, remember, and transmit his learning from one generation to the next—man has attained an unsurpassed dominance in the living world. It is also man's mind that permits his appraisal of the animals that share the world with him and that allows him to assume the standards by which others may be judged as strange.

The animals described in these pages are grouped by biomes, the major habitat divisions of the biosphere. Often the distinctiveness of an animal is directly related to the ways developed by the species for survival in its particular biome or to the more narrow confines of some niche within the biome. Other groups or even species have, like man, a generalized adaptability enabling them to live in several or even in most of the major habitats. In this book, these groups or specific animals are placed in the biome with which they are most commonly associated. There are cases, too, where the description of a species may include relatives or similar but unrelated animals that have developed identical or comparable features though they live in totally different biomes. These are clearly indicated.

The seas comprise the largest and most continuous of the biomes, covering some 71 percent of the earth's surface with a single salty envelope that occupies 90 percent of the Southern Hemisphere and 60 percent of the Northern Hemisphere. Despite the immensity of this watery world, the seas offer a remarkably uniform habitat in which there are only minor variations in saltiness. The variations in temperature, pressure, light, currents, and other physical factors are great over the expanse of the seas, but in any particular location or stratum, the seas change only in small degree from day to day or from season to season, much less so than any other biome. The seas are primarily the domain of the fishes among the vertebrates, but all other classes of vertebrates, except the amphibians, are represented there as well.

Only about 1 percent of the water on earth is fresh, and most of this is locked unusably for living things in the snow and ice at the poles or on the peaks of high mountains. But the remaining fresh waters—lakes, ponds, rivers, streams, swamps, and wetlands—teem with living creatures. Again, the fishes dominate, for they are the only truly aquatic vertebrates, but the freshwater world is also the realm of the amphibians. All of the other vertebrate groups are well represented in this biome, too, which differs most strikingly from the seas in its great variation, not only from place to place but also from day to day and season to season.

The land biomes are broad belts of essentially like conditions around the world. The tropics and subtropics encircle the earth immediately north and south of the equator. Here the kinds of creatures are most diverse: that is, there is a greater variety of species here, but fewer members within each species. Although the tropics appear to be robust, this biome is actually the most fragile, the most easily and drastically harmed by man's tampering. Toward the poles both north and south are vast grassland areas—the pampas in South America,

▲ Arctic tern ▼ False vampire bat

▲ Yellow seahorse ▼ Meller's Indian chameleon

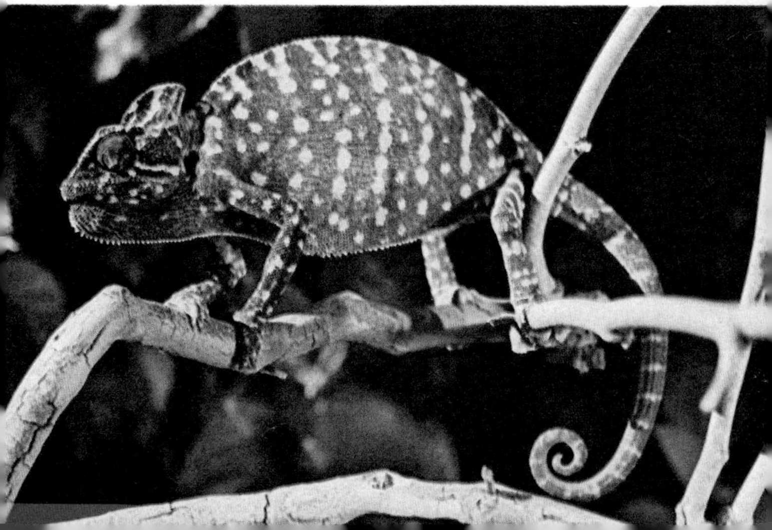

the savannas in Africa, the steppes in Asia, and the Great Plains in North America. In North America and Eurasia, the grasslands are now almost totally utilized by man for growing grain and for grazing cattle and sheep. The grasslands of South America, Africa, and Australia have been encroached upon similarly as man has altered the natural world to feed himself and his animals. Closely associated with the grasslands are the deserts—the dry lands, where the annual rainfall is less than ten inches (25.4 cm) per year, most of it coming in a very brief period. The living conditions of the deserts are hostile, not only because of dryness but also because of the extremes of temperature, and they necessitate very special adaptations.

Two forest belts also band the continents in temperate to cool climates. One is comprised of deciduous trees; the other, closer to the poles, is dominated by conifers. The deciduous forest biome is heavily populated by man and has, as a result, been largely destroyed everywhere in the world. Most forests today are secondary growths. The coniferous forests, despite the fact that they are the principal sources of the world's lumber, are larger and more intact. In the coniferous forest biome the summers are short, the winters long and severe. Toward the poles from the coniferous forests are lands of extreme cold and perpetual snow and ice. Antarctica is swept by strong, icy winds and is surrounded by cold seas. It has no connection to any other continent. The northern polar region, in contrast, has a direct land connection to continental heart-

▲ Leopard gecko

lands. North of the coniferous forests are the tundra lands in which the ground is permanently frozen except for a thin top layer that thaws briefly in summer. Then the tundra becomes bright with blossoms and green growth. Many kinds of animals move into the tundra in summer and then retreat to warmer climates in winter.

Mountains offer biomes in bands determined by altitude comparable to those based on latitude. On some of the world's highest mountains, as in the Himalayas that are based in the tropics, every biome is clearly seen. Depending on their location and height, others may show only one or two distinct strata. In this book, those animals that live at high altitudes where conditions are much like those in the polar regions are included with the polar animals. Most of these animals cannot, in fact, survive at lower elevations.

Still another distinct habitat consists of islands. The continental islands are those so close to the mainlands that their animal life is generally identical. But oceanic islands differ. Most of them volcanic in origin, they have been separated from the mainlands for so many years that they have evolved distinctive animal populations. Australia, sometimes referred to as the "island continent," is included with the islands in this book though it is large enough to have the same representation of biomes as larger continents. Its isolation, however, has resulted in a unique fauna, some of which is shared with nearby islands.

▲ Clown triggerfish

1

Tropics

Armadillo

Armadillos are the armored tanks among mammals, their bodies encased in bony plates with only a few scattered bristly hairs. Some kinds roll into a ball for protection. More than half a dozen species inhabit Central and South America.

The nine-banded armadillo (*Dasypus novemcinctus*) has spread northward into the United States and is now found from Texas to Florida. About three feet long (91.4 cm), with one-third of this length its scaly tail, the nine-banded armadillo appears to be neckless, and its large membranous ears look as though they were borrowed from a donkey. Its eyes are small and weak, but its sense of smell is well developed. A good swimmer, it gulps air to fill its intestines and give it additional buoyancy. Interestingly, this armadillo typically gives birth to identical quadruplets, the fertilized egg dividing twice to make four before the embryos begin development.

The giant armadillo (*Priodontes giganteus*), from Brazil, may measure more than four feet long (1.2 m) and weigh as much as 125 pounds (56.7 kg). Along with other armadillos, it belongs to the same group as anteaters: the edentates, or toothless mammals. But like all armadillos, it does have primitive, peglike teeth—a hundred of them, more than any other mammal. The third toe on each front foot bears an enormous

◀ Tropical rain forest, Africa

claw, the longest in the animal kingdom in relation to the size of the animal. This is used to tear apart ant and termite nests.

Basilisk

The toes of these iguanid lizards of the American tropics are fringed along the sides. When alarmed, a basilisk (*Basiliscus sp.*) stands on its hind legs and runs with great speed, even across the surface of water without sinking in. Males have a saillike crest that extends from their head to the tip of their tail.

Blind Snake

Snakes of about a hundred species in half a dozen families (Leptotyphlopidae, Typhlopidae, and others) are either wholly blind or nearly so, their eyes reduced to pigmented spots that function only to distinguish light from dark. Because of their secretive habits, these snakes are seldom seen and their habits are not well known. All are burrowers, and typically they have a wormlike head and smooth, shiny scales. Many of the species also have a cornified spine at the tip of the tail, incorrectly believed by some to be a poisonous stinger. Blind snakes feed on worms, ants, termites, and other small animals that live in the soil.

Caecilian *(pronounced See-sil-e-en)*

These legless and blind burrowing amphibians look like giant earthworms. The greater percentage of the approximately seventy-five species live in Central and South America. Even where they are locally abundant, however, caecilians, the most primitive of all the amphibians, are so secretive they are seldom seen. Some are small—only about six inches long (15.2 cm); the largest measures four and a half feet (1.4 m). Most secrete a slime that covers their body and is an irritant to would-be predators. Unlike most amphibians, the females coil around their eggs to help incubate them.

Chameleon

The more than eighty species of chameleons range in size from the two-foot (61-cm) Oustalet's chameleon *(Chamaeleo oustaleti)* to the one-and-a-half-inch (3.8-cm) dwarf chameleons

▲ Nine-banded armadillo ▼ Blind snake

▼ Basilisk ▼ Caecilian

(Evoluticauda sp.), both found in Madagascar. True chameleons are found only in the Old World, most of them in central and southern Africa. (The lizards commonly called chameleons in the United States are anoles, members of the iguanid family.) Chameleons can change color, but the range of colors is much more limited than stories have it. They can change from light to dark, as from tan to green or black, and they may also gain or lose spots. They cannot arrive at perfect matches for their background unless it happens to be in this general range.

Chameleons have even more remarkable features, however. Their eyes, for example, are on turretlike bumps and can be moved independently, perhaps one looking straight ahead and the other scanning the leaves or branches below. Equally unusual is the chameleon's tongue, which has a sticky, club-shaped tip and in most species is longer than the lizard's head and body combined. The chameleon uncoils and shoots out its tongue with lightning speed and accuracy to get its insect

▲ Chameleon catching insect with tongue

prey. Chameleons are slow, deliberate climbers, their toes united in separate and opposable bundles that give them a firm, almost mittenlike grip. On the ground a chameleon is nearly helpless, however. Its long prehensile tail is carried in a coil when it is not wrapped around an object.

Cuban Tree Frog

The largest tree frog in the United States, a big female measuring eight inches (20.3 cm) or more in length with her legs extended, the Cuban tree frog (*Hyla septentrionalis*) was recorded in Key West before 1900 and may have been introduced at different places in Florida many times over the years. It is a native of the American subtropics.

The population of Cuban tree frogs in the United States is now well established in the Miami area. Because of its size and insatiable appetite, it has in many areas eaten into oblivion the smaller, bird-voiced, native tree frogs. In years when it is especially abundant, the Cuban tree frog creates a more unusual problem, for it causes numerous power failures. Apparently mistaking high-voltage buzzes for the similar sounds made by bugs, it stands on transformers and stretches toward the noise, flicks out its tongue, and presto!—there is a flash as the transformer is shorted and the lights go out. Whole substations have been knocked out of operation temporarily by this pesky frog, necessitating a tripling of troubleshooting crews at times of pest abundance. The big frogs also enter houses by dropping down bathroom vents to get into darkness when dawn catches them on a rooftop, or they make flying leaps through open doors. Either way, they cause great consternation and sometimes near hysteria when they are discovered as cold, clammy blobs among the towels or bed linen or when, having stuffed themselves into the overflow drains of sinks, they peer out when somebody bends over to brush his teeth or wash his face.

Outside at night, the calls, screams, and bleats of a few dozen Cuban tree frogs around a house can be almost deafening. The caustic slime covering the skin of Cuban tree frogs is sufficiently irritating to cause dogs, cats, and other predators to avoid them.

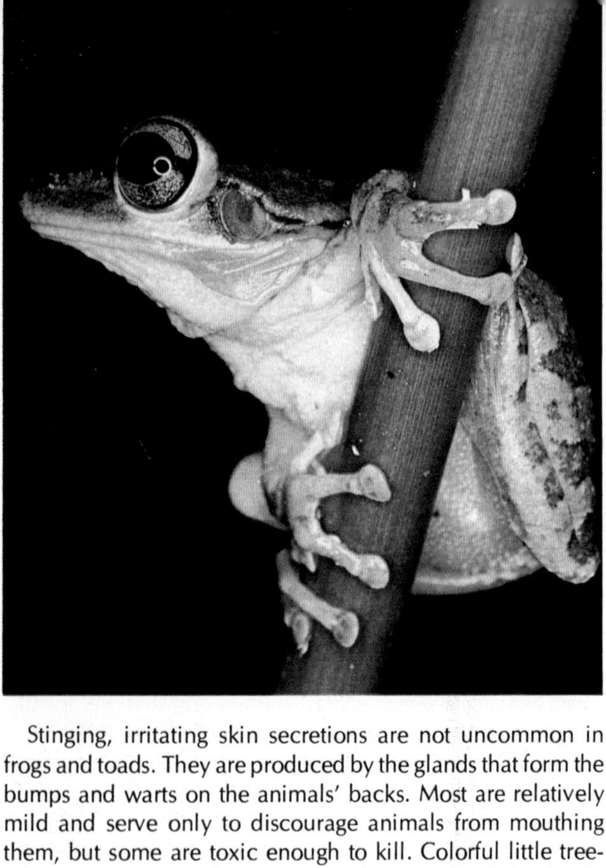

Stinging, irritating skin secretions are not uncommon in frogs and toads. They are produced by the glands that form the bumps and warts on the animals' backs. Most are relatively mild and serve only to discourage animals from mouthing them, but some are toxic enough to kill. Colorful little tree-inhabiting frogs of South America are the source of the deadly curare which the Indians use to tip their darts and arrows. In such a concentrated dosage, the toxin can cause instant death in monkeys and even humans.

Another poisonous amphibian of the American subtropics is the marine toad (which see).

Egg-Eating Snake

Many kinds of snakes eat eggs, swallowing them whole and digesting the shells and their contents. Most manage to constrict their bodies to break the shells once they are in the stomach, but African egg-eating snakes *(Dasypeltis sp.)* are so peculiarly adapted for eating eggs that they constitute the

▲ Cuban tree frog

snakes' whole diet. Further, they eat only the contents of the eggs and reject the shells.

Most egg-eating snakes are less than two feet long (61 cm) and are not much bigger in circumference than a man's finger, but they can stretch their mouth around eggs the size of a chicken's or a duck's. Spiny projections from the neck vertebrae extend into the snake's gullet and act as a saw to cut through the shell as it is forced into the throat. As soon as the shell collapses and the fluid contents run into the stomach, the snake regurgitates the shell and its membranes.

Elephant

Elephants are such familiar beasts that their uniqueness is almost ignored. They are, of course, the largest of all living land animals. The Asian elephant *(Elephas maximus)* has small triangular ears, a humped back, a single finger at the end of its trunk, and relatively small tusks. The males stand about ten feet tall (3 m) at the shoulders and weigh six tons (5,443.2 kg). The African elephant *(Loxodonta africana)* is more sway-backed and has large fanlike ears, two fingers at the end of the trunk, and large tusks. Males may stand eleven feet tall (3.3 m) at the shoulders and weigh up to seven tons (6,350.4 kg).

An elephant's tusks are greatly enlarged incisor teeth. In a large bull African elephant, the tusks may measure more than eleven feet long and weigh about two hundred pounds (90.7 kg) each. They are solid ivory. Elephants use their tusks not only for defense but also for rooting and for uplifting trees and bushes. An elephant's molar teeth are equally unusual. Normally there is only one molar on each side in both the upper and lower jaws, but behind each tooth there is a replacement ready to grow in as the old tooth wears away. In its lifetime, an elephant has a total of twenty-four molars, five replacements for each of the originals. Each molar weighs about nine pounds (4 kg) and measures about a foot wide and a foot long, its top corrugated with ridges.

Elephants are vegetarians, an adult consuming about a quarter of a ton of fruit, leaves, and branches daily. It also drinks great quantities of water, about fifty gallons (189.2 l) every day. The water is first drawn into the trunk and then squirted into the throat. The trunk's capacity is about two gallons (7.6 l). An elephant's trunk is actually a greatly elongated and mobile nose, double-tubed and with the nostril openings at the tip. The trunk weighs as much as 250 pounds (113.4 kg) and is controlled by an intricate set of muscles, powerful enough to lift logs and yet sensitive enough to pick up a tiny twig. The trunk is also used for making loud trumpeting calls, or an elephant may walk underwater in a lake or a stream and stick its trunk above the surface like a snorkel. If an elephant goes into deeper water, it swims—and with astonishing ease for such a giant and nonaquatic animal. The elephant's sense of smell is acute, but it has small eyes and relatively poor vision.

Flying Dragon

Living in the tropical forests of southeastern Asia, these eight- to ten-inch (20.3–25.4-cm) agamid lizards *(Draco sp.)* have developed a remarkable means of moving from tree to tree. They glide. Loose folds of skin between their front and hind legs are spread into thin membranes when the lizards leap from the trunk or branch of a tree. The membranes are stiffened by lifting six or seven greatly elongated ribs. In most species the scales on the body are not unusual or striking in color, generally a mottled gray, brown, and black that provides camouflage against the bark, but the "wings" are bright orange or yellow with black stripes.

Flying Lemur

Flying lemurs *(Cynocephalus sp.)* are the largest and most adept of the gliding mammals, the two similar species living in southeastern Asia and in the Philippines. The gliding membrane extends not only between the front and hind feet but also from the front feet to the neck and from the hind feet to the tip of the tail. Even the toes are webbed. About the size of domestic cats, flying lemurs, also called colugos or cobegos, can jump from the top of a tree and glide to the next, sometimes spanning distances of several hundred yards in a single glide. When they land on the trunk of a tree, they seem literally to disappear, their grayish black-and-white mottled fur blending with the bark in perfect camouflage.

Flying Snake

A three-foot-long (91.4-cm) tree-dwelling snake of southeastern Asia, the flying snake *(Chrysopelea pelias* and others*)* may launch itself from the top of a tree and glide to another, always moving downward but managing to keep the angle of drop at about 45 degrees to achieve distance. In its glides, the snake spreads or flattens its body and holds itself rigid. The ability of the flying snake to glide is unquestioned, but many of the tales told about the distance of their glides and their ability to maneuver in midair are exaggerations.

Gecko

A gecko can walk across a ceiling or even up a pane of glass, but it does not have suction pads on its toes. Instead its toe

▲ African elephant

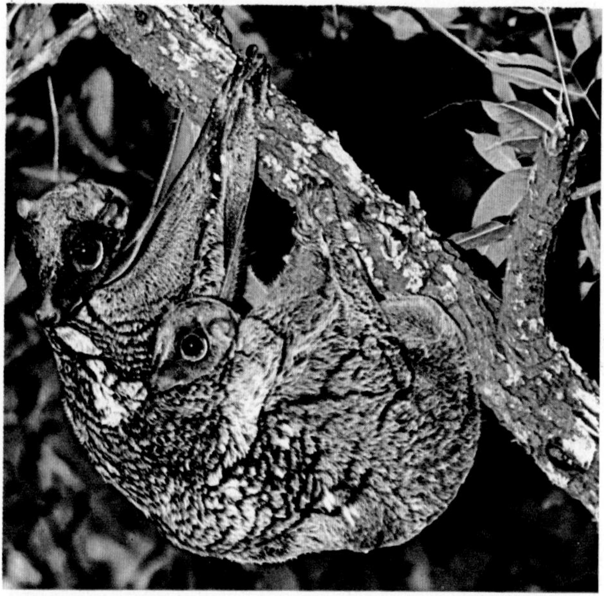

pads are divided into a number of horizontal plates, the surfaces of which consist of numerous hooked cells whose minute irregularities catch onto whatever they contact. The toes end in sharp claws that are equally useful in climbing trees. In at least one African group the tip of the tail also has a pad of clinging structures similar to those on the toes. The tails of geckos as a group are remarkably diverse, in fact. Some taper like a typical lizard's tail, but in an Australian species *(Phyllurus cornutos)* the tail is widened and leaflike. In others the tail is short and fat. The tail of a Central American species *(Thecadactylus rapicaudus)* is so plump that the lizard's common name is turnip-tailed gecko, and an Australian variety *(Nephrurus sp.)* with a peculiar enlargement at the tip of its tail is called the kidney-tailed gecko. As in many lizards, a gecko's tail breaks off easily and is commonly shed voluntarily. A new tail, similar to but often shorter than the old one, grows to replace it. If the old tail breaks incompletely, a new tail may grow anyhow, resulting in a two-tailed gecko.

▲ Flying lemur and young

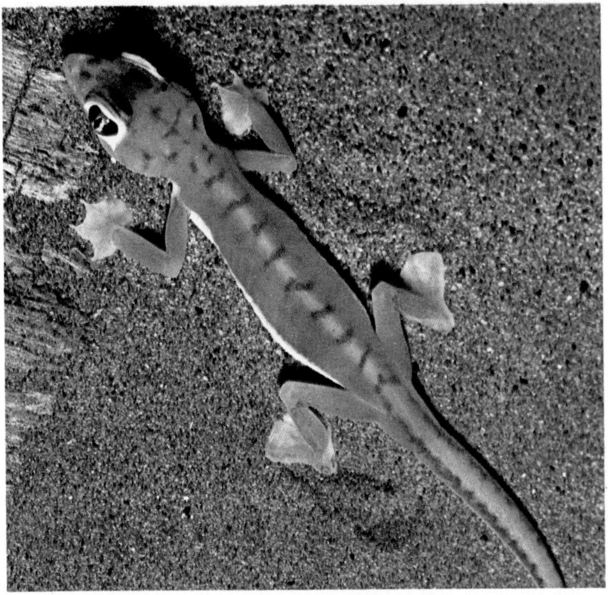

Unlike other lizards, geckos make noises—screeches, clicks, chirps, hoarse croaks, bleats. The calls are so distinctive, in fact, that each species can be identified by its sounds. Geckos also have unique eyes. Most are active at night, and during the day their large pupils are reduced to slim slits. In some the pupils are lobed, and when they contract, multiple images are superimposed on the retina, resulting in a much brighter and more sharply formed image than would be obtained from one large aperture. Unlike other lizards, most geckos do not have movable eyelids.

About three hundred species of geckos occur in all types of habitats around the world, from sandy deserts to dense forests. Some kinds favor living in houses, where they endear themselves by making meals of cockroaches, flies, mosquitoes, and other house pests. A few measure six to eight inches in length, but most are only about four inches (10.2 cm) long. The tokay *(Gekko gecko)* of southeastern Asia is the largest of all the geckos, attaining a length of twelve inches (30.5 cm) or more.

▲ Web-footed gecko

Giant Anteater

The giant anteater *(Myrmecophaga tridactyla)* is toothless, and because the claws on its front feet are so long, it walks on its knuckles or on the sides of its feet. Reaching lengths of up to eight feet (2.4 m), with its hairy tail accounting for half its length, the giant anteater may weigh as much as fifty pounds (22.8 kg). It makes its meals of ants and termites, and when it finds a nest, it uses its powerful claws to rip it apart, then pokes in its long, narrow snout and begins picking up the insects, eggs, and larvae with its sticky tongue. The tongue may be as much as a foot and a half long (45.7 cm).

The giant anteater is a ground dweller. It lives in the American tropics, as do two other species of anteaters that are primarily tree dwellers. They are the silky or two-toed anteater *(Cyclopes didactylus)*, about one and a half feet long, and the short-haired tamandua *(Tamandua tetradactyla)*, as much as four feet long (1.2 m) and with a naked, prehensile tail.

Giant Flying Squirrel

Like the smaller flying squirrels that live in the woodlands of North America and Europe, the giant flying squirrel *(Petaurista philippensis)* is actually a glider rather than a true flier. It spreads the thin membrane between its front and hind legs to make a gliding surface and is reported to have been airborne for as much as a quarter of a mile (402.3 m). About the size of a domestic cat, the giant flying squirrel inhabits the tropical forests of southeastern Asia.

Hoatzin *(pronounced Ho-at-sin)*
Looking more like some prehistoric reptile than a modern-day bird, a young and still-naked hoatzin *(Opisthocomus hoazin)* climbs among the branches of the shrubby trees around its nest, using the claws on the first and second digits of its wings as well as its feet and its bill. If the chick falls into the water—the poorly built nests of sticks are frequently over a stream—the little bird swims to a tree and climbs back up to safety. After a few weeks, its unusual wing claws disappear.

Hoatzins give off a peculiarly reptilelike musky odor, and internally their extremely large crop occupies most of the front of the body. In this enlarged sac, digestion of the tough and rubbery leaves of the tropical shrubs and trees on which it feeds begins. About the size of a chicken, the adults are unable to fly well, for their flight muscles as well as the bony keel to which they are attached are greatly reduced. They manage only to glide from branch to branch. Restricted to northeastern South America, the hoatzin does indeed appear to be a curious link with reptilian ancestors.

◀ Giant anteater ▲ Giant flying squirrel

Honey Guide

Like the European cuckoos, the thrush-sized honey guide *(Indicator indicator)* of Africa does not build a nest but instead lays its eggs in the nests of other birds. A newly hatched honey guide has a sharp hook at the tip of its bill which it uses to dispatch any other young that hatch from the eggs in the nest. The hook drops off when the bird is about a week old. Honey guides are insect eaters, and most of the species specialize in eating the larvae and eggs of bees and wasps, their thick skin providing some protection from stings when they rob a nest. They also consume large quantities of wax, which is digested by bacteria in their intestines.

When a honey guide finds a nest of wild bees, it calls loudly and flutters its wings noisily. It may even search for a honey badger, or ratel, and perform where it can be seen. It then leads the honey badger back to the nest. The honey guide waits while the mammal tears apart the nest, and when the honey badger has had its fill, the bird moves in for its feast. African natives in search of honey also follow the honey guide to nests, and they always leave some for the birds, superstitiously fearful of what ills might befall them if they do not.

Hoopoe *(pronounced Hoo-poo)*

The size of a mockingbird, the hoopoe *(Upupa epops)* wears a crest of black-tipped feathers that look like an Indian's headdress, and it has an exceptionally slim bill for probing in debris to get the grubs, worms, and other small animals that make its meals. The hoopoe is noted for its filthy nest and also for its

strong, almost skunklike body odor, quite in contrast to the bird's handsome appearance. Hoopoes live in the forests of southern Europe, Africa, and Asia.

Hornbill

Hornbills *(Buceros sp.)* not only have long bills, almost as big as those of toucans, but also have bony casques covering the top of their head externally. Both bill and casque are hollow or have numerous air-filled pockets. An exception is a Brazilian species in which both the bill and helmet are as solid as ivory. Hornbills mate for life. They nest in hollow trees, and when the female goes inside to lay her eggs, the male seals the opening with mud. In most species, the female works from inside the cavity to help with the sealing. They leave only a slit wide enough for the female's bill so that she can reach out to get the food carried to her by her mate or so that he can drop it inside. The female also drops excrement, inedible seeds, and other wastes out through the slit.

Protected from monkeys, snakes, and other predators, the female incubates her eggs and stays inside with her chicks until they are feathered and nearly fully grown. For most species this self-imposed imprisonment lasts for about three months. When the time comes for her to emerge with her young, both the cock and the hen work at chipping away the

◀ Hoopoe ▲ Hornbill

plaster-hard mud. From her months of inactivity and the constant feeding by the male, the female is fat and out of condition, and has difficulty flying at first.

Hornbills live in the forests of tropical and subtropical Africa, southeastern Asia, and nearby islands. All of the forty-five species are large birds, several as much as five feet long (1.5 m) from the tip of the bill to the tip of the tail.

Horned Frog

The South American or Brazilian horned frog *(Ceratophrys ornata)* is the most beautiful of all frogs, its rich brown body swirled with green and accented by dots of yellow and white and by reddish bars. A short triangular "horn" of skin projects over each eye. But the horned frog's beauty is only skin deep. This eight-inch (20.3-cm) toad is the most pugnacious of all amphibians. It eats other amphibians, small rodents, and birds, and fearlessly attacks animals much larger than itself—even dogs, men, and horses. It is not poisonous, but it bites hard and holds on tenaciously.

Howler Monkey

These monkeys *(Alouatta sp.)* take first place for loudness in the monkey clan. Their voice boxes are greatly enlarged, their throats expanded with goiterlike pouches to accommodate the noisemaking apparatus. When howlers scream, their voices sometimes carry for a distance of three miles (4.8 km). A troop of howlers traveling through the treetops can sound like an approaching storm. Several species of howlers live in the American tropics, some at elevations of five thousand feet (1,524 m) or higher in the mountains.

Hummingbird

The more than three hundred species of hummingbirds, forming the family Trochilidae, are all natives of the New World, ranging in distribution from the southern tip of South America to Canada and from the steamy tropics to the windswept heights of the Andes. It is in the subtropics and tropics that they are most abundant and varied. Hummingbirds are indeed the
 gems of the bird world, their plumage iridescent and occurring

in almost every conceivable color and combination. The various species wear all types of feather adornments, from crests and collars to pendent plumes. The largest hummingbird, more than eight inches long (20.3 cm), is the giant hummingbird *(Patagona gigas)* that lives in the Andes. The smallest, only slightly more than two inches long (5 cm) including its bill and tail, is the Cuban bee hummingbird *(Mellisuga helenae).* All hummingbirds are aggressive, almost belligerent.

Like the closely related swifts, hummingbirds have tiny feet. They can perch but are not able to walk. In flight, they are unequaled in the bird world. Their wings beat so rapidly they make a humming noise. In all except the largest species, the wings can be seen only as a blur, and they may vibrate at two hundred beats per second in full flight. Speeds of up to sixty miles per hour (96.5 km/hr) have been reported for hummingbirds, but most scientists say this is an exaggeration and thirty miles per hour (48.3 km/hr) is more accurate. The endurance of hummingbirds is unquestioned, however. The tiny ruby-throated hummingbird *(Archilochus colubris),* only three and a half inches long (8.9 cm), travels across the Gulf of Mexico between North and South America on migration flights, requiring five hundred miles (804.5 km) of nonstop flying over the water. Before launching on this journey, the little bird wisely fuels its body, adding as much as 50 percent to its normal weight.

▲ Black howler monkey ▲ Broad-billed hummingbird

Hummingbirds are also masters at maneuvering. Not only can they fly forward with bulletlike speed but also backward, up, or down, and they can hover—literally standing still in midair. Their powerful flight muscles account for at least a quarter of their total weight. Hummingbirds eat nectar, sipping it from deep-throated flowers by inserting their slim, pointed beaks. This rich sugar diet gives the tiny birds the great energy they need for flying. Many also consume the ants or other small insects that are feeding on the nectar, too.

In some hummingbird species, the male's courtship ritual is one of the most spectacular sights in nature. After he has established his territory, the male lures a female by zooming back and forth before her in a wide arc—going high in the air, pausing, and then swooping down and back up again as though on a swing. Some hummingbirds mate while in flight.

Female hummingbirds build the nests, which are the smallest, most intricate and delicate of all nests in the bird world. Woven of spider silk, moss, and plant down, the nest is a tiny cup in which the female lays two eggs, those of the smallest hummingbirds about a quarter of an inch long (6.3 mm).

Jaçana *(pronounced: Zha-sin-a)*
Living along the shores of lakes and streams in tropics throughout the world, the seven species of this aquatic bird (family Jacanidae) are distinguished by their extraordinarily long toes and flattened claws, an adaptation that enables them to walk with ease on the leaves of hyacinths or water lilies without sinking in. Jaçanas also have a sharp spur at the bend of each wing and use them as weapons in battles.

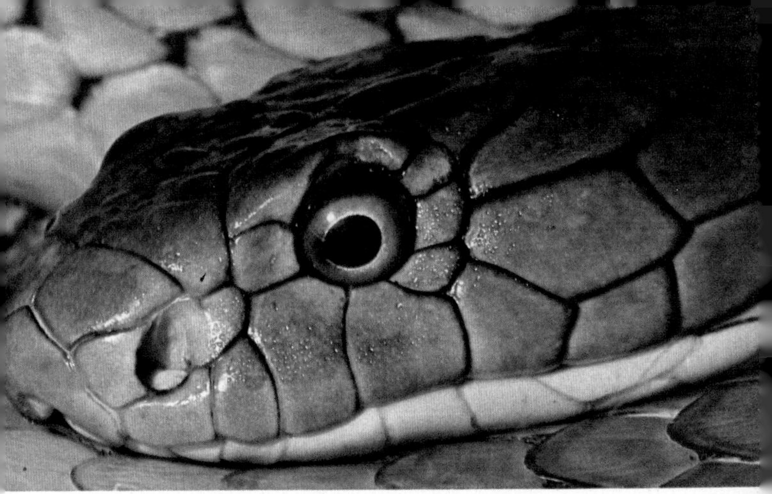

King Cobra

A giant among snakes, known to reach a length of eighteen feet (5.5 m) though usually shorter, the king cobra *(Ophiophagus hannah)* is extravagantly endowed with potent venom, equipped with the power to kill an elephant though its usual fare is rats and mice. A large cobra may contain enough venom to kill as many as thirty men. Before attacking, a cobra lifts the front of its body and flattens its neck to form the characteristic hood. The hood of the Indian or spectacled cobra *(Naja naja)* bears a pair of black spectaclelike markings that folklore explains as the finger marks of Buddha, who blessed the cobra for spreading its hood and shielding his eyes from the sun while he napped. The Indian cobra, smaller than the king cobra, is responsible for about 25 percent of the thirty thousand annual deaths due to snakebite in India, because this cobra frequents houses in its search for rats and mice and also lies in the warm, dusty trails along which people walk barefoot.

In addition to the king and Indian cobras, half a dozen other species of cobras inhabit southeastern Asia, and an equal number of species occur in northern Africa. Among them is the asp or Egyptian cobra *(Naja haje)*, believed to be the species used by Cleopatra in committing suicide. The spitting cobras (which see) have the most unusual method of ejecting their venom.

◀ Jaçana ▲ King cobra

Close relatives of cobras, equally dangerous but lacking hoods, are the three- to four-foot (91.4-cm–1.2-m) kraits (pronounced krites) of southeastern Asia, the Indian krait *(Bungarus caeruleus)* actually responsible for almost as many deaths per year as the Indian cobra. In equatorial Africa, the slim tree-dwelling mambas *(Dendroaspis sp.),* some to nearly fifteen feet long (4.6 m), are easily disturbed, attacking quickly and silently.

In the United States, the two species of coral snakes *(Micrurus sp.)* belong to the same family as the cobras and deliver a neurotoxic poison of equivalent potency. Almost a dozen species of coral snakes are found also in South America.

The cobra family is most generously represented in Australia and New Guinea. In Australia, eighty-five species, or 60 percent of all the kinds of snakes there, are poisonous, more than a dozen of them highly lethal. Among the most deadly of these are the death adder *(Acanthophis antarcticus),* taipan *(Oxyuranus scutellatus),* and tiger snake *(Notechis scutatus).* The tiger snake is said to have the most deadly venom, drop for drop, of all snakes in the world.

Marine Toad

The largest of the true toads and one of the giants among present-day amphibians, the marine toad's body *(Bufo marinus)* measures eight to nine inches long (20.3–22.8 cm), and it may weigh more than a pound (453.6 g). Noted for its voracious appetite, the marine toad consumes vast quantities

▲ Marine toad

of insects, and because of its size it can reach high on a plant to get its prey. For this reason the marine toad has been introduced to many farm regions in warm areas around the world for the biological control of insect pests.

The burgeoning population of marine toads in southern Florida apparently got its start when a shipment of the toads escaped from crates at Miami International Airport. Each female lays thirty thousand to forty thousand eggs every breeding season, so the toads soon became abundant. Their help in controlling pests is appreciated, but the marine toad is also poisonous, the warty patches on its back secreting a substance known as bufotoxin that is potent enough to kill a medium-sized dog.

Though marine toads are primarily insect eaters, they also eat fruit and garbage with equal zest, and they have been known to steal food put out for pets.

Marmoset

Among the most attractive of all monkeys, marmosets *(Callithrix sp., Cebuella sp., Leontocebus sp.)* have long, brightly colored, silky hair. This makes them among the most appealing of the monkeys exhibited in zoos, and the marmosets seem to enjoy being looked at. They talk constantly in high birdlike chirps and trills that have been deciphered as a fairly precise monkey language. What most zoo visitors do not realize is that these beautiful little monkeys can also communicate with ultrasonic sounds, and so even in moments of seeming si-

▲ Golden marmoset

lence, marmosets are making noises that only they can hear.

Marmosets, which inhabit Central and South America, are the smallest of all monkeys, few of them as big as squirrels. The pygmy marmoset *(Cebuella pygmaea)* is only six inches long (15.2 cm).

Mousebird

Mousebirds, or colies, of six species (family Coliidae) live in the forests of southern Africa. They are slim birds, their tail twice as long as their body, and their plumage is grayish and soft, literally mouselike in appearance. Mousebirds also resemble rodents in the way they run along the ground or creep through the branches. Their outer toe on each foot swivels, so that it can be pointed either forward or backward and thus becomes equally useful in climbing either up or down a tree or in hanging from a branch.

Oilbird

Emerging from its daytime hideaway deep in caves, where it clings to the wall like a swift, the oilbird *(Steatornis caripensis)* sets out at dusk to feed. Like a bat, it finds its way in the dark by a system of echolocation, the only bird to do so. Its sounds, however, are of a much lower frequency, distinctly audible to the human ear. The oilbird's body measures only about thirteen inches long (33 cm), but it has a wingspread of two and a half feet (76.2 cm). Because its diet consists only of the oily fruit of palm trees, the oilbird's flesh has an extremely high fat content. Sometimes the birds may travel forty or fifty miles (64.3–80.4 km) from their roost to find the fruit, then return before daybreak.

Speckled mousebird ▲ Rufous ovenbird ▶

Oilbirds make nests of their own droppings, consisting largely of the undigested palm seeds. The naked young are fed copious amounts of the oily palm fruit, and because of their inactivity, they gain weight rapidly, soon weighing twice as much as their parents. When the young lose their second set of down feathers and get regular flight feathers, they begin to slim quickly to the proportions of their parents.

Guacharo is a local name for the oilbird, which lives in northern South America and on the island of Trinidad.

Oropendola *(pronounced O-ro-**pen**-do-la)*

Oropendolas (*Zarhynus sp., Gymnostinops sp.,* and others) build unusual socklike nests, some as much as six feet long (1.8 m). These birds nest in colonies, so dozens of these skillfully woven sacks may be suspended from the branches of one tree. These relatives of orioles live in Central and South America.

Ovenbird

Ovenbirds—more than two hundred species ranging throughout Central and South America—build a unique nest that accounts for their name. The dome-shaped structure of the rufous ovenbird *(Furnarius rufus)* is made of mud or clay bound together with roots and stems. The opening to the nest is on the side, and the chamber in which the eggs are laid is lined with grass. Some ovenbirds burrow in banks to nest; others nest in the cavities of trees or in rocky crevices.

A wood warbler of eastern North America builds a similarly shaped nest woven of grasses, twigs, and other plant materials. The nest blends so well with its surroundings that it is difficult to see. This bird is called an ovenbird, too.

Pangolin

Pangolins, or scaly anteaters *(Manis sp.)*, have large, overlapping scales covering their back, legs, and tail. If disturbed or threatened, they roll into a ball. Their head is relatively small, their tongue long and sticky. They have no external ears, and their nostrils can be completely closed—both features protect them against the biting insects on which they feed. All pangolins (four species in Africa, three in Asia) are similar in general body features and in habits. The largest is the giant pangolin *(Manis gigantea)* of Africa; it may be six feet long (1.8 m) and weigh sixty pounds (27.2 kg) or more.

Pangolins have large claws on their front feet for digging into ant and termite nests. The claws make walking difficult, and so the terrestrial pangolins turn their front feet on their sides or sometimes walk on their hind feet. Most pangolins climb trees and feed on the ants or other insects found there. Holding on with their hind feet and using their tail as a prop, these skilled climbers can swing the front of their body at right angles to the trunk of a tree to reach out-of-the-way branches.

Parrot

Parrots, macaws, parakeets, cockatoos, and their kin, a total of more than three hundred species, are among the most colorful of all birds. They inhabit the tropics around the world. Pygmy parrots *(Micropsitta sp.)* of New Zealand are less than four inches long (10.2 cm); the giant macaws *(Ara sp., Anodorhynchus sp.,* and others*)* of South America may be three and a half feet tall (1 m). One reason these birds are such popular pets is that they "talk." Some species are much more accomplished than others, but some are totally unable to mimic human speech. In the wild they make liberal and loud use of their own language, but "talking" is developed through their association with man and his repetition of words and phrases.

 Unusual among birds, parrots and their relatives use their

feet like hands, even holding food in one foot and biting off pieces. New Zealand's kakapo *(Strigops habroptilus)* is flightless, although it uses its wings for gliding. It spends most of its time on the ground, where it runs rapidly. It can also climb. Because it is active mainly at night, other names for it are owl parrot and night parrot.

Quetzal

The most striking of all the trogons, a family of highly colorful and ornamented birds of the American tropics and subtropics, the quetzal *(Pharomachrus mocino)* lives in the rain forests on mountains in Mexico and Central America. About the size of a

▲ Tree pangolin ▼ Amazon parrot ▼ Quetzal

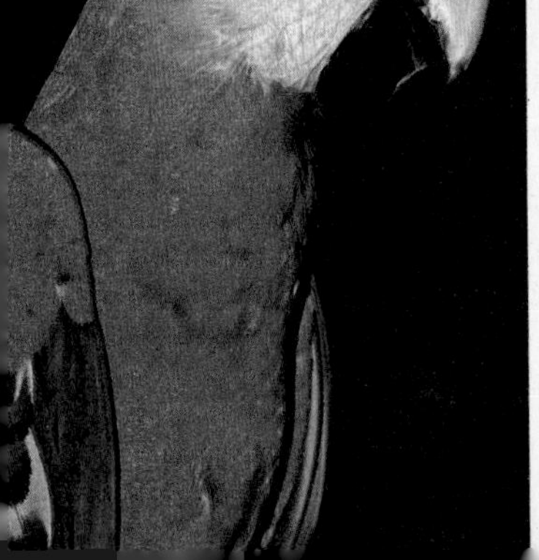

dove but with a tail fully two feet long (61 cm), the quetzal is basically metallic green with a scarlet belly and a black back. The tail feathers are white below, the long plumes a bronze green.

The beautiful quetzal is the national bird of Guatemala and is said by some to be the most gorgeous bird in the world. It was revered by the Indians who lived in the area long before the arrival of the Europeans, and it was the inspiration for Quetzalcoatl, the god of the Toltecs. The Indians plucked the tail feathers for use as decorations but did not kill the birds. The Spaniards and others who followed them were less wise and nearly exterminated the birds in the greedy harvest of the handsome plumes.

Sloth

The slowest of all mammals, sloths move along the branches of trees hanging upside-down, holding on with their long, curved claws. It is virtually impossible to dislodge a sloth from its hold on a branch. Even in death it continues to hang in its usual position. The sloth's toes are completely hidden in skin, with only the claws protruding. On the ground a sloth is nearly helpless, dragging itself slowly and getting back into a tree as quickly as possible.

Much of the sloth's life is spent sleeping, either holding tightly to a branch or anchored in a fork or crotch of a tree. The sloth's long, coarse hair hangs down from its back, lying in the

▲ Two-toed sloth

opposite direction from other mammals' hair. Often the hair is greenish because of growths of algae.

Two species of sloths live in the American tropics: the three-toed *(Bradypus tridactylus)* and the two-toed *(Choloepus didactylus)*. The three-toed sloth has a special fondness for the leaves and fruit of the cecropia tree and may spend its entire life in one tree.

Spitting Cobra

The African black-necked or spitting cobra *(Hemachatus haemachatus)*, to seven feet long (2 m), has the remarkable ability to spit or eject venom with deadly accuracy up to distances of six feet (1.8 m), aiming for its victim's eyes. The cobra may actually spit up to twelve feet (3.6 m) but generally misses its mark at this distance. It may eject half a dozen or more jets of venom before its supply is exhausted, but it is ready again within a day. The venom is harmless on the skin, unless there are cuts, but in the eyes it is painful and may cause blindness. The spitting cobra is a close relative of the king cobra (which see).

Swiftlet

Swiftlets *(Collocalia sp.)* are small swifts that live in caves in Asia and on offshore islands. They have enlarged salivary glands and produce saliva in such great amounts that their nests consist almost totally of the dried saliva. The nests of one

▲ Spitting cobra

species are so pure they are harvested commercially for use in making bird's-nest soup, an Oriental delicacy. Though it has an abundance of saliva, a swiftlet may work for a month or longer to build its nest.

Toucan

A toucan's bill may be as big as its body, and though it appears to be unwieldy and heavy, it is honeycombed with air spaces that make it lightweight and is manipulated with skill by the birds in eating fruit. Admittedly, a smaller bill would do as well. The toucan's bill, in many species strikingly colored as well as awesome in size, in one of nature's extravagances that is quite unexplainable in terms of the bird's needs today. Toucans *(Rhamphastos sp., Pteroglossus sp.,* and *Andigena sp.)* inhabit the forests of tropical and subtropical Central and South America.

Vampire

The most feared of all bats, vampires (family Desmodontidae) feed only on blood. With razor-sharp front teeth, they make small incisions in the skin of their victims and then lap up the blood that oozes from the wound. This is done with such

deftness that a victim may not even awaken from its sleep. Vampires make their attacks only at night, and in Central and South America, where they are abundant, their constant feeding can seriously weaken cattle, horses, and other domestic animals. Attacks on humans are rare, but where the bats are numerous and they cannot be shut out at night, a light may be kept on to discourage their approach. The largest of the vampires has a wingspread of about twelve inches (30.5 cm).

Worm Lizard

Worm lizards, or amphisbenids, look like big, blunt earthworms, the mimicry extending even to rings around the nearly cylindrical body. None of the approximately one hundred species has hind legs, and only three of the species have front legs, which are tiny and useless. Worm lizards do not have external ears, and in nearly all the eyes are covered with skin, showing through in some species as black dots. Like the earthworms they resemble, worm lizards stay underground in burrows, feeding on worms, insects, and other small animals. These most unusual of all lizards live in Africa and South America. Only one, the pinkish, twelve-inch (30.5-cm) Florida worm lizard *(Rhineura floridana)*, occurs in the United States. Most worm lizards are less than ten inches long (25.4 cm), but one South American species reaches a length of two and a half feet (76.2 cm).

◀ Short-billed toucan (far left), vampire bat (left) ▲ Worm lizard

2

Grasslands

Aardvark

Aardvark is an Afrikaans word meaning "earth pig," an apt name for this strange pig-sized mammal *(Orycteropus afer)* with erect, donkeylike ears on its narrow pig-snouted head. The mouth is small and tubular, and the sticky, wormlike tongue may be a foot and a half long (45.7 cm). The thick-rooted, sharply tapered tail is used as a prop when the animal sits, kangaroo-style, on its hindquarters. The aardvark uses the powerful claws on its front and hind feet to tear apart termite nests, then catches the scurrying insects with its tongue.

Aardvarks dig large burrows, big enough for a man to crawl into. To escape intruders, they dig with great speed, faster than several men with shovels could. An aardvark is almost toothless, having only molars that are rootless, lack enamel, and consist of a number of tiny tubes.

Cape Buffalo

Rated as the most dangerous of all animals, the untamable Cape buffalo *(Syncerus caffer)* may weigh a ton (907.2 kg) and stand five feet tall (1.5 m) at its shoulders. Its curved horns have a spread of nearly five feet, their tips arced upward broadly and the bases meeting on top of the head to form a solid "boss." Herds of these beasts are avoided even by lions.

◀ Amboseli Game Reserve, Kenya

The similar arna or water buffalo *(Bubalus bubalis)* that lives in southeastern Asia has even longer horns, measuring about six and a half feet (2 m) along their curve. But the arna has a much more gentle disposition and is used as a draft animal in many countries.

Cheetah

Also called the hunting leopard, the cheetah *(Acinonyx jubatus)* is a long-legged doglike cat, nearly six feet long (1.8 m) and weighing as much as 125 pounds (56.7 kg). Big cats typically roar, and small cats purr. But the cheetah chirps, howls, and barks. Unlike other cats, too, a cheetah cannot fully retract its claws into sheaths.

For short distances, a cheetah is the fastest runner in the animal kingdom, capable of attaining a speed of about forty miles per hour (64.4 km/hr) within two seconds and reaching a top speed of seventy miles per hour (112.6 km/hr). The easily tamed cheetah was once trained by sportsmen for use in hunting in much the same manner as falcons. The principal quarry was the fleet blackbuck, which the cheetah could overtake on short runs. Cheetahs are natives of Africa and southern Asia, but their numbers have been so greatly reduced that they are now near extinction.

Giraffe

The tallest of all animals, a giraffe *(Giraffa camelopardalis)* can browse on leaves as much as eighteen feet off the ground. Standing twelve feet tall (3.6 m) at the shoulders, a giraffe obtains the additional stretch with its long neck. (Despite its length, a giraffe's neck contains only seven vertebrae, the same as a human's.) As a further aid, the giraffe's tongue may be a foot and a half long (45.7 cm), and its hairy lips are mobile. While this exceptional height is of great advantage in feeding beyond the reach of other browsers, it makes bending down to drink quite difficult. To do so, the giraffe must spread its legs wide apart, and in this awkward straddled position it is most vulnerable to attackers. In running, a giraffe brings both legs on the same side forward simultaneously, giving it a peculiar rolling gait. A giraffe has short, knobby, skin-covered

▲ Aardvark ▲ Cheetah

▲ Cape buffalo ▼ Giraffes

horns—usually four, but occasionally five. Though essentially quiet, giraffes do make occasional grunts and squeaky noises, some of which may be beyond the range of human hearing. The several varieties of giraffes are distinguished by their color and pattern. All live in the African savannas and bush country. A newborn giraffe is a diminutive replica of its parents and is able to walk within an hour after it is born.

Gnu

Also called the wildebeest, the gnu *(Connochaetes taurinus)* is the oddest of all the African antelopes. It is said to have the tail of a horse, ponylike hindquarters, the head and shoulders of a buffalo, the flattened muzzle of a moose, and the bristly beard of a goat. Both the males and females have thick, long, curved horns. Despite its awkward, ungainly appearance, the gnu is agile, and it has the unusual habit of making twisting leaps, as though it has been stung by a bee.

Jackrabbit

This swift and high-jumping mammal of the western United States measures only about a foot and a half long (45.7 cm) and weighs no more than ten pounds (4.5 kg), yet jackrabbits *(Lepus sp.)* have been clocked at forty-five miles per hour (72.4 km/hr), can hurdle fences eight feet high (2.4 m), and make horizontal leaps of twenty-five feet (7.6 m). Jackrabbits are hares, distinguished from true rabbits not only by their speed and jumping but also in giving birth to well-furred young that have their eyes open.

Klipspringer

Ranked as nature's highest jumper, this little African antelope *(Oreotragus oreotragus)*, which weighs only about twenty pounds (9 kg) and stands little more than eighteen inches tall (45.7 cm) at the shoulders, is reportedly able to make vertical leaps of twenty-five feet (7.6 m) to get onto a rocky perch. It can land on a spot not much bigger than a silver dollar.

Two other African antelopes, the springbok *(Antidorcas marsupialis)* and the impala *(Aepyceros melampus)*, are known for their leaping ability. Impalas can make horizontal jumps of thirty-five to forty feet (10.6–12.2 m).

Ostrich

The largest and most powerful of all living birds, an ostrich *(Struthio camelus)* may stand eight feet tall (2.4 m) and weigh over three hundred pounds (136 kg). It can maintain a running speed of twenty-five miles per hour (40.2 km/hr) for long distances, but it cannot fly, its small wings useful only in helping the bird brake its speed or in making turns. Two of the digits on each wing have sharp claws that are used as weapons in fights. The long and nearly featherless legs end in two-toed feet. An ostrich's mighty kick is said to be more powerful than a mule's, making it dangerous even to a lion. The long neck is almost featherless; the head is relatively small compared with the size of the body, the bill flat and rounded across the top.

◀ Jackrabbit (far left), klipspringer (left) ▲ Ostrich

When angered, an ostrich hisses and makes throaty roars. Contrary to popular belief, it does not bury its head in the sand.

Ostrich eggs are the largest laid by any living bird, though their size—eight inches long (20.3 cm), with a weight of three pounds (1.4 kg)—is not exceptional in relation to the size of the bird. Each female lays about a dozen eggs in a hollow scraped in the sand, and sometimes several females use the same nest. The males do most of the incubating.

Ostriches range over much of Africa but are most abundant in the open grasslands of northern Africa and southwestern Asia. They are omnivorous, eating small animals as readily as they do plants. They also have the unfortunate habit of swallowing inedible items, particularly shiny objects. A stomach analysis of an ostrich, especially a captive, is likely to turn up anything from rings and watches to bottles and golf balls.

Oxpecker

These African starlings *(Buphagus africanus)* feed on the ticks they find on the hides of rhinos and other big mammals of the savannas. They eat not only the ticks but also the blood that comes from the wound where the tick was attached. Whether the big animals, which include domestic cattle, understand this service is not known, but they do not seem bothered as the birds climb about over them. Oxpeckers are so specialized in their feeding habits that they will not eat any other kind of food and are not found where ticks have been eliminated by chemicals in domestic herds.

Oxpecker on warthog ▲ Saiga ▲ Raccoonlike dog ▶

Raccoonlike Dog

The raccoonlike dog *(Nyctereutes procyonides),* found in grasslands along waterways in Japan, Korea, and China, has a black mask over its eyes like the North American raccoon, and has short legs and a short, bushy tail. It is indeed the most undoglike in appearance of all wild dogs. The raccoonlike dog is now rare, having been heavily hunted for its fur, which is sold as "Japanese fox."

Saiga

An almost sheeplike antelope living on the Asian steppes, the saiga *(Saiga tatarica)* has a puffy bulbous or saclike nose that protrudes beyond its mouth and looks like a sawed-off elephant's trunk. The function of this grotesque structure is still debated, most scientists assuming that it warms cold air before it is taken into the lungs and that it may also act as a dust filter.

Sandhill Crane

Cranes are well known for their courtship dances, but of all the species, the sandhill crane *(Grus canadensis)* of North America seems to do its dances as much for sheer pleasure as for sexual or courtship display. Sometimes a whole flock of sandhill cranes performs simultaneously, some leaping as high as twenty feet (6 m) with their wings half spread. They may also throw sticks into the air and strike at them with their bills as they fall to the ground.

Secretary Bird

Laws in Africa protect this long-legged bird because of its penchant for killing cobras and other snakes. Standing as much as four feet tall (1.2 m), its legs covered with black

▼ Weaver building nest ▲ Warthog ▼ Secretary bird

feathers from the knees up, and wearing a pendent crest of grayish-black feathers, the secretary bird *(Sagittarius serpentarius)* differs from its hawk relatives in doing its hunting on foot. With one foot it knocks down a snake in striking position, then it batters the reptile with its wings. If the snake does manage to strike, the secretary bird jumps back quickly, and even if the snake succeeds in biting, it generally gets only the bird's wing feathers, where the venom does no harm. In addition to snakes, the secretary bird eats lizards, rodents, insects, and other small animals. The secretary bird ranges throughout the savannas of Africa.

Warthog

So ugly it almost defies description, the warthog *(Phacochoerus aethiopicus)* bears large crusty warts on its misshapen and broad-muzzled head. Its sickle-shaped tusks may be two feet long (61 cm), curving out and upward from its upper jaws. In its lower jaws, the tusks are broadly triangular, sharp, and about six inches long (15.2 cm). The warthog's dirty-gray skin is nearly naked, with only a few stout bristles here and there. A thick mane extends down the midline of the back. Weighing to two hundred pounds (90.7 kg) and about six and a half feet long (2 m) including its tail, the warthog is long-legged and can run fast, holding its tail stiffly erect. When rooting for food, it commonly shuffles along on its knees. The warthog is widely distributed in the African savannas.

Weaver

Belonging to the Old World finch family and represented most abundantly in the savannas of Africa, the weavers *(Philetairus socius)* are mostly social birds, known for their complex condominiumlike nests that may house hundreds of families. These nests may be ten or fifteen feet tall (3–4.5 m) and equally large in diameter.

Widowbirds *(Vidua sp.)*, members of the same family and occurring in the same area, do not build nests. Rather, the females lay their eggs in the nests of other birds, as cuckoos do. The females are inconspicuous, but the males in breeding plumage have exceptionally long tails.

3

Deserts

Camel

Famed for their ability to go long periods without water (actually, however, they must have water every few days), camels do not store water in their humps except possibly indirectly. Their humps—one in the Arabian, or dromedary *(Camelus dromedarius),* two in the Bactrian *(Camelus bactrianus)*—are used for storing fat, which is utilized when rations are sparse. The humps of well-fed camels, therefore, are full and rounded, those of underfed camels less prominent or firm. When this fat is broken down for use in the body, some of it may be converted into water metabolically.

In the deserts of northern Africa and Asia Minor, camels have served as beasts of burden for centuries and were probably the first animals ever domesticated. Despite this long association with man, camels are extremely stubborn and have a nasty habit of spitting and biting. The Arabian camel no longer exists in the wild, and only a few Bactrian camels are found wild, probably feral, in the Gobi Desert.

For transportation across the deserts, camels have no equal. Each animal can carry a load of five hundred pounds (227 kg) or more and may travel as much as forty miles (64.4 km) per day. The camel walks with a rolling gait, both legs on a side moving forward at the same time. Remarkably adapted for its life in the desert, a camel's two-toed feet spread wide to give it

◀ Death Valley, California

firm footing in the loose sand. Its exceptionally long eyelids serve as screens to keep out sand, and its nostrils can be closed. Its mobile lips, the upper one split or lobed, are thick for grasping the coarse desert plants on which the camel browses.

Chuckwalla

Almost eighteen inches long (45.7 cm), the chuckwalla *(Sauromalus obesus)* is a chunky-bodied iguanid lizard that lives in the deserts of the American Southwest. It makes its meals of cactus flowers, favoring the yellow ones, and succulent plants. At night it hides in crevices in the rocks. If a human or other animal attempts to remove it, the chuckwalla inflates its body to wedge itself in place. The Indians, who ate chuckwallas, used a pointed stick to deflate the lizard's body so that it could be removed.

Gila Monster

The only poisonous lizards in the world are the gila monster *(Heloderma suspectum)* of the southwestern United States and adjacent Mexico and the closely related and very similar Mexican beaded lizard *(Heloderma horridum)* that is found only in Mexico. Both have thick bodies, beady eyes, a thick tail, and short, stout legs. Their scales do not overlap but fit one

▲ Gila monster ▼ Chuckwalla

against the other in beadlike rows. These slow-moving lizards use their sense of smell in tracking down prey, detecting odors by rhythmically flicking out their tongue in a snakelike manner. Their diet consists primarily of the eggs and young of ground-nesting birds, but they do not refuse any easily caught small animal. When food is plentiful, the short tail becomes a fatty reserve. When food is scarce, this fat is utilized, and the tail becomes thin.

The poison glands of both lizards are located in the lower jaw rather than in the upper jaw as in snakes, and the teeth of both jaws are grooved for transmitting the venom into the wound. First, however, the venom must move along a groove between the lower jaw and the lip to reach the grooved teeth. This mechanism is far less sophisticated than the hypodermic-like fangs of most poisonous snakes. The lizard grabs its victims and holds them in the remarkably powerful viselike grip of its jaws while waiting for the venom to flow along the channels and down the grooved teeth. The venom is essen-

◀ Arabian camel (dromedary)

tially a neurotoxin, causing death by paralyzing the victim's respiratory mechanism. Both lizards are dangerous but are not aggressive unless intruded upon. Arizona has passed a law to protect the gila monster, which in recent years has become rare.

Horned Lizard

Commonly called horned toads, these desert-dwelling lizards *(Phrynosoma sp.)* of Central and North America have a squat, flattened toadlike shape, enabling them to bury themselves easily in the sand to escape the hot sun. They accomplish this with great speed, going down belly-first by tilting themselves first to one side and pushing into the sand, then repeating the movement with the other side. Each time they also push sand over their back by flicking their tail. They may also dig in head-first.

Most horned lizards have horny spines on their back and tail, those down the midline prominent but the largest on the back and sides of the head. They resemble the moloch (which see) of the Old World but are a bit less grotesquely armored. When disturbed or angered, a horned lizard puffs its body and bulges its eyes, ejecting several drops of blood from ruptured blood vessels.

▲ Naked mole rat ▼ Jerboa

Jerboa

Jerboas *(Jaculus sp.)* are long-tailed, medium-sized rodents that live in the deserts of northern Africa, southern Russia, and Mongolia. Sand-colored, perfectly camouflaged in their habitat, jerboas can survive without drinking water, getting all they need from the succulent plants they eat. They have powerful hind legs for jumping and can easily leap ten feet and occasionally as much as fifteen feet (3–4.5 m).

Naked Mole Rat

Inhabiting Somaliland and northern Kenya, the naked mole rat *(Heterocephalus glaber)* is earless and completely naked except for a scattering of hairs over its body. It lives in sandy soil, in which it burrows to feed on bulbs, roots, and other underground parts of plants. The naked mole rat is about five inches long (12.7 cm), including its inch-long tail.

◀ Horned lizard

Poor-Will

The poor-will *(Phalaenoptilus nuttallii)* of western North America is the only bird known to hibernate in winter. Like other members of its family—about sixty species of nightjars widely distributed in temperate and tropical regions—the poor-will feeds almost exclusively on insects which it catches in flight. With the coming of winter, this food disappears—and so do the poor-wills. Scientists scoffed at the tales told by Indians of birds that spent the winter sleeping in crevices in cliffs, and it was not until the 1950s that investigators verified their stories. The poor-wills tuck themselves deep into rocky niches and do not emerge until spring. As in all true hibernators, their metabolic rate decreases. Their body temperature, for example, drops from 102° F (38.9° C) to 65° F (18.3° C).

All of the insect-eating nightjars have exceptionally wide mouths, and nearly all have bristly feathers at the corners of the mouth to help them in trapping insects. The male nighthawk *(Chordeiles minor),* a widely distributed North American nightjar, performs unusual aerial dives in courting his mate, zooming down from high in the sky straight toward his mate on the ground and pulling out of the dive daringly close to the ground. The air makes a loud buzzing noise as it rushes through his wing feathers. Most nightjars will also move either their eggs or their young at the slightest sign of danger.

Roadrunner

As big as a bantam chicken, the roadrunner or chaparral cock *(Geococcyx californianus),* a member of the cuckoo family, can run fifteen miles an hour or faster (24 km/hr) across the scrubby desert country of the American Southwest in pursuit of the lizards, snakes, and other small animals on which it feeds. As it runs, the roadrunner's small wings are held out half opened, and its long tail serves as a balancer. A roadrunner beats its catch to death with its beak and then swallows it whole and head-first.

Sidewinder

The sidewinder *(Crotalus cerastes),* an eighteen- to thirty-inch (45.7–76.2-cm) rattlesnake of the American Southwest and Mexico, has distinct earlike "horns" over its eyes, and it moves through the loose sand with a sidewise motion. It accomplishes this by moving first one and then another lateral loop of its body forward, its direction of movement oblique or at an angle. This unusual type of movement is shared with several species of true vipers *(Vipera sp.)* living in the deserts of northern Africa. The sidewinder is a pit viper (which see).

◀ Roadrunner ▲ Sidewinder

4

Forests

Bat

Bats (order Chiroptera) are the only winged mammals capable of true flight, some two thousand species inhabiting temperate and tropical regions around the world. Among mammals, they rank just below rodents in number of kinds represented.

A bat's wings are thin membranes stretched between the greatly elongated "fingers" of its front legs and extending also between the front and hind legs. The hind feet are free. Though their flight pattern often appears "floppy" or erratic, bats are capable of covering hundreds of miles on their migration flights.

Bats are not blind, but the tiny eyes of the abundant insectivorous bats are probably useful only in distinguishing day from night. Some bats, particularly the fruit bats (family Pteropodidae), do have large and functional eyes. Those lacking useful eyes find their way in the dark by a remarkable radarlike system called echolocation. In addition to making easily heard mouselike squeaks, these bats emit sound pulses at a frequency of 50,000 to 100,000 cycles per second, well above the range that can be heard by the human ear. When these pulses strike objects, they echo back to the bat and are interpreted with amazing accuracy to determine the location of the object from which they were bounced. For picking up

◀ Evergreen forest at Nymph Lake, Colorado

these sounds, some bats have exceptionally large ears, many with extra earlet lobes or folds. Horseshoe bats (family Rhinolophidae) also have complex folds of skin over the nose, forming a wrinkled mass between the nose and the eyés. These also help in picking up the sound echoes. Vampires and a few other kinds of bats have complicated ear folds or leaflike noses. It is most astonishing that bats can not only judge the position of the objects ahead, but they can also determine such details as its size and whether it is dead or alive. Using echolocation, for example, a bat may swoop down in flight and pluck an insect from the leaf of a tree.

Bats sleep during the day, hanging head-downward while holding onto a branch, leaf, rock, or other object with their hind feet. Those that live in temperate regions either hibernate in winter, collecting in large numbers in caves, hollow trees, or buildings, or they migrate southward as winter approaches.

Most bats give birth to a single young, which clings to the mother and accompanies her even on hunting trips until it is about two months old. The most familiar bats are the insect eaters, but one species that lives in the American tropics specializes in catching fish, skimming the surface of bays and ponds and grabbing small fish with its sharp claws. Vampires (which see) feed exclusively on blood. Other kinds have a diet of fruit and nectar.

Box Turtle

Box turtles *(Terrapene sp.)* belong to the freshwater turtle family but have become land-dwellers, like the tortoises. In the process, these timid and otherwise defenseless turtles have evolved a highly effective means of protection from intruders: they can draw their head, neck, legs, and tail completely inside their shell and then shut it so tightly that it cannot be opened except by breaking it. The belly plate, or plastron, is hinged both at the front and rear to make this total closing possible, and the top shell, or carapace, is highly arched, providing the space inside to accommodate the head, neck, and appendages. After its retreat, a box turtle waits patiently until all becomes quiet, then opens the front of its shell slightly and peeks out. If the danger seems passed, the turtle opens its shell more, but still cautiously. Finally it sticks out its legs and goes on its way.

People sometimes carve their initials in the lower shells of box turtles, and pranksters occasionally forge names and dates—such as "G.W., 1775"—to try to establish a phenomenal age for a turtle. But sufficient authenticated records exist without these tricksters to indicate that box turtles do become centenarians with regularity.

Crossbill

Crossbills *(Loxia sp.)* are so named because their upper and lower mandibles do literally cross, forming tweezerlike instruments used to extract seeds from pine cones. These birds belong to the same family as cardinals, buntings, and sparrows, and they live in the coniferous forests of North America, Europe, and Asia.

◀ Lesser horseshoe bat ▲ Box turtle

Cuckoo

Old World cuckoos, some forty species in the family Cuculidae, never build nests of their own but always make certain their young are given good foster care. At egg-laying time, the female puts each of her eggs in the nest of some other bird, generally selecting one whose eggs are similar in size and color to her own. Often she watches as the couple she intends to dupe build their nest, and she may move in to lay her egg on the same day that her host lays her first egg. Typically the cuckoo takes one egg out of the nest and holds it in her bill while she deposits her own in the same spot. Then she flies off with the stolen egg and, at some distance away, drops it, sometimes eating the contents. Within a two-day period, she may lay four or five eggs, each in a different nest.

Cuckoo eggs hatch in about twelve days, which means that the naked and very demanding cuckoo hatchling is almost always the first young in the nest. Immediately it begins shoving out the remaining eggs or hatchlings, if any, until it is the sole occupant, getting the full and devoted attention of its foster parents. Any that survive the first three or four days of jostling are accepted without further squabble, but a young cuckoo is so aggressive, fast-growing, and voracious that it may starve its nest companions by getting all of the food brought by the parents. The young cuckoo is soon larger than its stepparents, who labor to keep it fed until it is fully feathered and departs to live on its own.

Fire-bellied toad ▲ Glass snake ▶

European Mole Rat

The European mole rat *(Spalax hungaricus)* burrows like a mole but uses its wedge-shaped muzzle and head and its teeth to cut its way through the dirt. Its eyes are tiny, functionless, and covered with skin, and its ears are greatly reduced in size. This shovel-headed rodent, which ranges into northern Africa and southwestern Asia as well as in Europe, digs elaborate underground living quarters, with storage galleries, mating and nursery chambers, resting areas, and latrines.

Fire-Bellied Toad

This ordinarily inconspicuous, grayish, four-inch (10.2-cm) European toad *(Bombina bombina)* becomes a different creature when threatened. Lying on its belly, it arches both its head and its rear end upward while at the same time turning the undersides of its arms and legs upward. This exposes bright red undersurfaces, a warning to attackers. If this signal is not heeded and the toad is mouthed, the predator learns its lesson, for the secretions coating the toad's body will burn the attacker's mouth.

Glass Snake

A glass snake *(Ophisaurus sp.)* cannot, as folk tales would have it, break its body into several pieces and then put itself back together. A glass snake does, however, have an exceptionally

long tail, often twice as long as its body, that snaps off if grabbed. The detached tail, which sometimes breaks into more than one segment, continues to wriggle, presumably satisfying an attacker while the head and body crawl off. In time, a new tail grows to replace the lost one.

Glass snakes are most abundant in the American tropics, but several species are found also in Europe and Asia. They are not really snakes but legless lizards, having only rudimentary and functionless legs near the anus. The largest is the scheltopusik *(Ophisaurus apodes)*, which lives in southern Europe and southwestern Asia; it reaches a length of four feet (1.2 m) and is thick-bodied, making its meals of mice, lizards, and other small vertebrates. Most glass snakes are two feet or less in length (61 cm), and they eat worms or other invertebrates.

Hedgehog

Hedgehogs have a round, seemingly neckless body covered with short, sharp spines. They defend themselves by rolling into a ball and presenting only their uplifted spines to an intruder.

Weighing only a little more than a pound (453.6 g) and measuring about ten inches long (25.4 cm), the several species

▲ European hedgehog

of hedgehogs live in Europe, Asia, and Africa. The common European hedgehog *(Erinaceus europaeus)* is famed for its immunity to the venom of vipers, the only poisonous snakes in Europe. Hedgehogs make meals of these snakes, thus earning the appreciation of farmers and gardeners. Hedgehogs also eat insects, worms, snails, birds and their eggs, and other small animals, and they occasionally eat fruit. An ancient legend in Europe tells of hedgehogs impaling apples on their spines and then carrying them to their burrows to store them for winter food. This, of course, is a myth, but hedgehogs have been observed with apples or other fruit on their spines, possibly there are as a result of the animals' rolling on the fruit.

Hognosed Snake

The most famous bluffers among snakes, the flabby-bodied hognosed snakes *(Heterodon sp.)* of the eastern United States employ two ruses on intruders. First the snake will try to scare a would-be attacker. By lifting its long ribs and stretching its loose skin over them, it flattens its body. Rising part way off the ground and looking almost cobralike, it sways, hisses, and strikes—but, interestingly, it never opens its mouth. If this is not sufficient to send a foe scurrying, the hognosed snake then

▲ Hognosed snake

rolls onto its back and writhes, at the same time opening its mouth and letting its tongue loll out. Finally the seemingly dying snake becomes still, lying on its back and "playing dead" so convincingly that it will flop back again if turned onto its belly. When all becomes quiet, the snake lifts its head and looks around cautiously. If there are no signs of danger, it rolls onto its belly and goes on its way.

Hognosed snakes get their name from their turned-up, hog-like snout, which they use in burrowing through loose sand and debris. Toads are their principal food, but they may also eat frogs, other reptiles, and insects.

Ivory-Billed and Pileated Woodpeckers

The largest of the world's woodpeckers, both the ivory-billed *(Campephilus principalis)* and the pileated *(Dryocopus pileatis)* measure more than a foot and a half (45.7 cm). The pileated is still fairly common in the forests of the southeastern

Pileated woodpecker ▲ Lemming ▶

United States. The ivory-billed, once abundant in the same area as well as in Cuba, is believed to be extinct now, as is the very similar and equally large Mexican imperial woodpecker. These big birds depended on large dead trees in the forests for their homes and as sources of food, and these trees have been destroyed, no longer left standing even in commercial forests.

These crow-sized woodpeckers are distinguished not only by their big bills but also by their prominent and colorful crests. Their barbed and sticky tongues extend as much as three inches beyond the tip of the bill, enabling the birds to extract insects from deep inside burrows after they have chiseled a hole into the wood to get them. The sound of a pileated woodpecker hammering on a tree may carry for a mile or more through the forest. The bill, as in all woodpeckers, is driven by a powerful set of neck muscles that also cushion the impact of the blows for the bird.

Lemming

The populations of lemmings *(Lemmus lemmus)* in the Scandinavian countries of northern Europe periodically "explode," the cyclic abundance generally occurring every three or four years. Scarcity of food forces the mouse-sized rodents

to migrate to find new supplies, and the moving hordes consume everything edible in their path. They do not, as stories have it, make a mass suicidal migration to the sea, but the movements are generally downhill and along the valleys that lead eventually to the sea. When the lemmings come to streams, lakes, or the sea, they do not turn back but rather attempt to swim across, and many drown in the large bodies of water. In addition, great numbers become victims of owls, hawks, foxes, and other predators that feast on the swarms of little animals.

Midwife Toad

The male midwife toad *(Alytes obstetricans),* a native of Europe, gets so involved in marital affairs that he becomes the custodian of the eggs. As the female lays her eggs and the male releases sperm on them, the long, sticky strands get wrapped around his hind legs. Thus entrapped, the male accepts his midwifery duties. During the day he hides in a hole or depression in the ground. At night he sallies forth to fill his stomach, and if the night is not damp enough to moisten the eggs with dew, he goes into the water to wet them. In about a month the eggs are ready to hatch, and this time when the male enters a pool, the larvae emerge from their eggs and swim off to complete their development.

Mole

Only slightly larger than mice, moles *(Scalopus sp.* and others) spend their entire lives in underground burrows that they dig with their large and powerful flipperlike front legs. The burrows may be as much as six feet underground (1.8 m), with a network of tunnels leading from the central nest. In loose soil they can dig with astonishing strength and speed, traveling as much as forty feet (12.2 m) in an hour. Moles are blind. The tiny eyes of most species are covered with skin, although they may in some cases serve to distinguish light from dark. A mole's hearing and sensitivity to vibrations is acute, however.

Moles are insectivorous, consuming grubs, ground-dwelling insects, worms, and other small creatures found below the surface. Some observers report that moles store

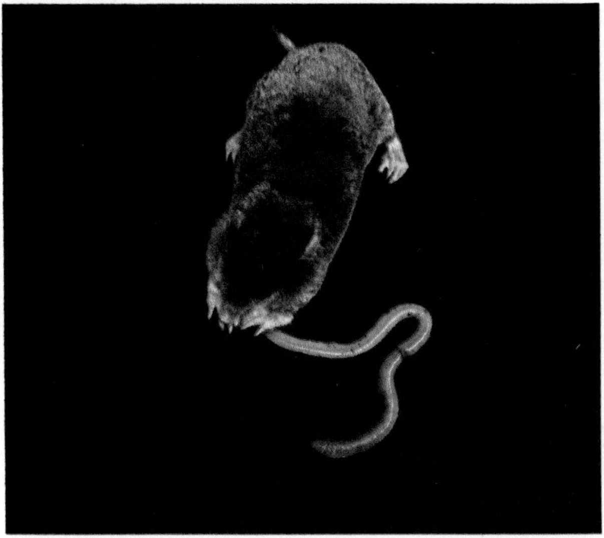

earthworms, immobilizing them by biting off the head end. Moles do not eat plants in flower and vegetable gardens, but they may upset the plants as they root through the soil in their search for small animals. Like shrews, they have hearty appetites and may consume their own weight in food every day.

Most moles have a long, flexible snout with sensory bristles near the tip. The snout of the unusual star-nosed mole *(Condylura cristata)* ends in a rosette of twenty-two fleshy feelers.

Mouth-Breeding Frog

Also called Darwin's dwarf frog because it was Charles Darwin who discovered this inch-long (2.5-cm) frog in the forests of southern South America, the mouth-breeding frog *(Rhinoderma darwini)* has the most unusual breeding habits of any amphibian. Several males stand guard over the dozen or so eggs laid by a female until they are almost ready to hatch. Then each male picks up several of the eggs, stuffing them into his vocal pouches. There the eggs hatch and the larvae complete their development, not emerging until they are fully grown froglets.

▲ Mole eating earthworm

Opossum

The common, American, or Virginia opossum *(Didelphis marsupialis)* is the only marsupial, or pouched mammal, native to North America. Marsupials are believed to have developed in the Americas but were later replaced by the placental mammals. Several close relatives of the common opossum live in South America, but marsupials are today most abundantly represented in the Australian region and include kangaroos and wallabies, the Tasmanian devil, the Tasmanian wolf or thylacine, flying phalangers, bandicoots, and the koala. In almost all marsupials, the young are born less then two weeks after conception. Still not fully developed, the newborns are blind, naked, and no bigger than kidney beans or honeybees. These tiny creatures crawl along a slimy track to the pouch, or marsupium, where each attaches itself by its mouth to a cup-like teat and then continues its development. A female opossum has thirteen teats, but she may give birth to more than twenty young. Those that do not find a nipple in the pouch do not survive. The still embryonic young cannot suck at first. The mother contracts her muscles to express milk into their mouths. In about two months, when they are more fully developed, they detach themselves from the nipples and begin moving around independently. Now they can suckle like any other young mammal. Young opossums often ride on their mother's back or cling to her scaly prehensile tail with their own grasping tail.

The common opossum is noted for feigning death when it is captured. It lies on its side, shuts its eyes, and opens its mouth, drooling and letting its tongue hang out. Sometimes it becomes so quiet that even its breathing cannot be detected. This habit was long interpreted as deliberate trickery. Recent studies indicate, however, that the death-feigning is probably a state of mild shock that the opossum enters when frightened.

Owl

Almost all of the more than 130 species of owls in the world, found everywhere except in the Antarctic, are nocturnal and have large eyes set on the front of their broad face. They are not blind during the day but neither are they comfortable in bright

light, either keeping their eyes shut or reducing the size of the pupils to slits. Owls have a well-developed sense of hearing, useful in detecting their prey in the darkness, and are nearly noiseless themselves in flight. Though they appear to be neckless, owls actually have rather long, flexible necks —in fact, an owl can turn its head 180 degrees. Owls prey on a wide variety of animals, particularly birds and rodents. Indigestible parts, such as bones, fur, and feathers, are regurgitated as pellets that are common around nesting areas.

Only a few kinds of owls actually hoot. The deepest and most sonorous of the owls is the great horned owl *(Bubo virginianus)*. Many kinds of owls give quavering, almost musical calls, and some screech and scream, their sounds unnervingly demoniacal. Many click their bills loudly in flight. Owls range in size from the Mexican elf owl *(Micrathene whitneyi)*, less than six inches long (15.2 cm), to the great horned owl, which stands more than two feet tall (61 cm).

Opossum ▲ Eagle owl ▲

Pit Viper

Pit vipers have a unique sensing mechanism marked externally by a deep pit between the nostril and the eye on each side of the head. A membrane at the bottom of the pit is richly supplied with nerves. This unusual organ detects heat—so accurately that a pit viper can locate its warm-blooded prey even in the dark. Some pit vipers are so sensitive to heat that they can put their head into a rodent's burrow and determine whether the occupant is there, or they can scan their detectors along a branch to discover whether a bird is at roost in the darkness.

With the exception of a few species in southeastern Asia and one species in extreme southeastern Europe, pit vipers are restricted to the Americas, where they are most diverse and abundant in warm regions. They include in North America the copperhead *(Ancistrodon contortrix)*, water moccasin or cottonmouth *(Ancistrodon piscivorus)*, and some twenty species of rattlesnakes *(Crotalus sp.* and *Sistrurus sp.)*; in Central and South America, the Mexican moccasin *(Ancistrodon bilineatus)*, fer-de-lance *(Bothrops lanceolatus)* and approximately twelve close relatives, bushmaster *(Lachasis mutus)*, and about two dozen species of rattlesnakes *(Crotalus sp.)*. The bushmaster is the largest of the pit vipers, reaching a length of twelve feet (3.6 m). Largest in the United States is the southern diamondback *(Crotalus adamanteus)*, known to exceed eight feet (2.4 m). The one with the most unusual method of locomotion is the desert-dwelling sidewinder (which see).

Porcupine

The spines or quills on a porcupine are a supplement to its covering of hair. Porcupines native to the Old World have thicker and longer spines, some exceeding eighteen inches in length (45.7 cm), than do those native to the New World. The common or Canadian porcupine *(Erethizon dorsatum)* has some twenty-five thousand to thirty thousand quills, and each quill, ranging from an inch to five inches long (2.5–12.7 cm), has as many as a thousand barbs. A porcupine does not shoot its quills, but it may strike an attacker by lashing its tail, always
 managing to embed many quills that work their way into the

victim's skin. They are drawn inward by the involuntary movement of the victim's muscles and have been known even to impale the heart.

Shrew

The shrews include the smallest and also the most voracious of all mammals. Tiniest of the more than 150 species is a musk shrew *(Suncus etruscus)* that lives in the Mediterranean region of Europe and Africa. Its body is less than two inches long (5 cm), its tail about an inch. This little shrew weighs less than a dime. The North American pygmy shrew *(Microsorex hoyi)* is only slightly larger. One of the largest and certainly the strongest is the so-called hero shrew *(Praesorex goliath)*, which lives in tropical Africa. Because of its interlocked vertebrae, this nine-inch (22.8-cm) animal is said to be able to support the weight of an average man on its back.

Shrews belong to the insectivore group of mammals, along with moles and hedgehogs. Though abundant in most areas, they are so secretive that they are seldom seen. Most shrews are active for about three hours and then rest for three hours, regardless of whether it is day or night. They make their meals of insects, worms, or any other small animals, commonly consuming more than their own weight in food every day. They will starve within a day, in fact, if they do not get food. Shrews attack savagely and can kill animals twice or more

their own size. Some secrete a potent poisonous saliva that can paralyze or kill mice and may be painful even to man. One species of shrew has a poison powerful enough to kill two hundred mice. Most kinds of shrews give off a musky odor that is offensive to attackers, though some predators ignore this smell. Because of their hyperactivity—a shrew's pulse exceeds a thousand beats per minute—shrews are short-lived, most of them dying when they are little more than a year old. Highly sensitive, they may be killed by a sudden loud noise, such as thunder, and unless handled gently and given a place to hide immediately, captives commonly die of shock.

Spadefoot Toad

Found on all continents except Australia and Antarctica, spadefoot toads *(Scaphiopus sp.* and others) have horny projections or "spades" on their feet. These are used for digging in the loose soil or sand, the toads actually sinking backward out of sight. Sometimes they burrow to a depth of two feet (61 cm) or more. During droughts, these toads may stay underground for months, emerging only when the surface is damp again.

Swift

Fastest of all birds, a spinetailed swift *(Chaetura sp.)* of eastern Asia is credited with a speed of two hundred miles per hour (321.8 km/hr). Like other swifts, it is so highly adapted to life on the wing that it may fly an entire night without resting and

▲ Spadefoot toad

even mate on the wing. All swifts have slim, pointed wings, a teardrop-shaped body, and a very small beak. The mouth gapes wide—to behind the eyes. Most have a short tail, the feathers ending in stiff spines, and their feet are so small and weak that most swifts cannot perch on branches as other birds do. With their sharp nails, and using their short, spiny tail as a prop, they cling to vertical surfaces such as rock faces, the hollows of trees, or chimneys. Most make nests of twigs, grass, feathers, or similar materials which they plaster to the vertical surfaces where they roost.

The long-tailed scissor-tailed swifts *(Panyptila sp.)* of Central and South America differ not only in perching on branches with regularity but also in making hanging tubular nests as much as two feet long (61 cm), broader at the top than at the bottom and suspended beneath a rock ledge, big branch, or under an eave. They enter the nest at the bottom and crawl up the tube to lay their eggs on a platform near the top. The African palm swift glues its eggs to a pad of feathers on a palm frond or some similar large leaf and incubates the eggs while clinging to the leaf itself. Crested swifts *(Hemiprocne sp.)* make even smaller nests, not much larger than those of hummingbirds. Only slightly larger than a half-dollar, the nests consist of no more than a pad of feathers and bark glued to a small branch at the top of a tree. A single egg is glued to the center of this nest. All swifts use copious amounts of saliva in fastening their nests together and to hold their eggs to the nests.

▲ Swift

5

Poles and High Mountains

Arctic Tern

Close relatives of gulls but generally smaller and more graceful in flight—often, in fact, called sea swallows—terns are further distinguished by their pointed "swallow" tails and by their slim, straight bills. The Arctic tern *(Sterna paradisaea)* holds the record in the bird world for annual migration distance. The birds breed in the Arctic and then winter along the coasts of extreme southern Africa and Antarctica. The annual round trip is about 22,000 miles, and most of the flight is across the open sea.

Condor

Condors, the largest of all present-day flying birds, are New World vultures, belonging to the same order as eagles and hawks. The Andean condor *(Vultur gryphus)* has a wingspread of nearly ten feet (3 m), and the California condor *(Gymnogyps californianus)* is only slightly smaller. The California condor is now near extinction. Many, because of their large size and slow flight, fell victim to gunners; others were poisoned by eating carcasses of animals killed with bait put out to exterminate vermin. In addition, their normal fare of wild animal carcasses was depleted as the land became settled. Still

◀ Mt. Everest, viewed from Khumbu Glacier, Nepal

another factor contributing to their decline, the females lay only one egg per year, and the birds do not breed until they are six years old.

Vultures are not beautiful, except perhaps the king vulture *(Sarcorhamphus papa)* of Central and South America. Like other vultures, the king vulture has a naked head, but its skin is bright yellow, green, purple, and red, and its plumage is a striking black and white. Condors and other vultures have reddish or black heads and necks, the Andean with grotesquely wrinkled wattles. All are masters at soaring, capable of riding thermals from sunup to sundown with scarcely a flap of their wings. The Andean condor has been seen soaring at altitudes of twenty thousand feet (6,705.6 m). Vultures are virtually voiceless, able only to make hissing noises. Both their beak and talons are so weak they cannot kill living prey or even feed easily on the flesh until it has been softened by decay. They have superb eyesight, however, and when one bird has found food it is soon joined by others. Whether their sense of smell is superior is still questioned, but it is definitely better than that of other birds.

Dipper

All four species of wrenlike dippers *(Cinclus sp.)*, widespread in both the New and Old worlds, live near mountain streams. They can swim and dive well, and they are commonly seen walking along the rocks at the very edge of the water. Most astonishing, a dipper, or water ouzel, simply walks into the water and disappears, seeming to continue to walk along the bottom. Actually it begins swimming as soon as it is submerged. The dipper's third eyelid, or nictitating membrane, is transparent, protecting its eyes while permitting it to see underwater. The third eyelid also shields the eyes from the spray and the splash of the fast-moving streams and waterfalls.

Musk Ox

The musk ox *(Ovibos moschatus)* survives on the near-barren lands of the Arctic, grazing on the vegetation that grows on the tundra in the short summer and then digging through the snow to get mosses and lichens during the winter. Despite this

▲ Arctic tern

▲ Andean condor ▼ Dipper

meager fare, the bulls attain a weight of seven hundred pounds (317.5 kg) and may stand four feet tall (1.2 m) at the shoulders. Cows are about one-third smaller. In the bleak and windy wastelands, the musk oxen are vulnerable to predators as well as to the cold. To protect their calves from wolves, a herd forms a tight circle with their heads turned outward toward the attackers and with the calves kept in the center. This makes them easy victims for hunters, however.

The musk ox wears a thick shaggy coat, and its short heavy horns meet in a boss on top of the head. More closely related to goats and sheep than to cattle, they have been given the name musk ox because of the strong musky odor produced by glands beneath their eyes. Sanctuaries have been provided to prevent the extermination of these unusual beasts.

Penguin

More than a dozen species of penguins live in the cold seas of the Southern Hemisphere. Two occur only in Antarctica. The most aquatic of all sea birds, penguins can swim at approximately twenty-five miles per hour (40.2 km/hr) underwater, propelling themselves with their webbed feet and their wings, which are actually featherless flippers. They literally "fly" underwater. At the surface they swim with their head above the water. Penguins can also explode from the water to a height of five or six feet (1.5–1.8 m) to land on an icy prec-

▲ Musk ox

ipice. They enjoy sliding on their bellies in the snow. On land they walk with an almost comical waddle. A penguin's feathers, barbless and almost scalelike, fit tightly against the body. Penguins assemble in large rookeries to lay their eggs.

Largest of the penguins is the emperor *(Aptenodytes forsteri),* which stands as much as four feet tall (1.2 m) and may weigh seventy-five pounds (34 kg). The king penguin spends its entire life on the icy coasts of Antarctica or in the cold surrounding seas. The female emperor penguin lays a single egg and then immediately returns to sea, leaving her egg in the male's charge. He holds the egg on his feet, snuggling it close to his body to keep it warm in temperatures that drop to -40° F (-40° C) and winds that may reach a hundred miles an hour (161 km/hr). He holds the egg for slightly more than two months, and when it finally hatches, the dutiful male has lost as much as a third of his weight. Miraculously, he still manages to regurgitate enough to feed the newly hatched chick for

▲ Adélie penguins

several days. Then the female returns—fat and vigorous, ready to relieve the male of his duties so that he can go out to sea to feed on shrimp, fish, or squid to gain back his weight and energy. The king penguin *(Aptenodytes patagonica)* shares this unusual incubation habit with the emperor penguin, but all other penguins make feather-lined nests in which the eggs are incubated in normal bird fashion.

Vicuña *(pronounced Vie-coo-nya)*
Inhabiting the high Andes, at fourteen thousand feet (4,267m) and above, the vicuña *(Vicugna vicugna)* not only wears a dense coat of fur to protect it from the cold but also has a greater number of red blood corpuscles than do animals living at lower elevations. Compared to man, for example, the vicuña has nearly three times more red blood cells, enabling it to get a maximum of oxygen even in the rarefied atmosphere. The vicuña can run twenty miles an hour (32.2 km/hr) or faster without tiring at elevations where man can scarcely get enough oxygen for survival.

The vicuña belongs to the same family as the camels of the Old World. Its other American relatives are the guanaco *(Lama guanicoe),* which lives at lower elevations, and the domesticated llamas *(Lama glama)* and alpacas *(Lama pacos),* used as pack animals and also valued for their fine, thick wool.

Yak

This shaggy beast wears the thickest and longest coat of hair of any mammal. The hair hangs down in a long skirt over the yak's legs and generally covers the eyes and ears. The tail is also bushy, and the underfur is thick and matted. One of the giants of the cow family, the yak *(Bos grunniens)* weighs as much as half a ton (453.6 kg) and may stand six feet tall (1.8 m) at the shoulders. It lives in the high mountain country of Tibet, occasionally to altitudes of twenty thousand feet (6,096 m). The yak is so totally adapted to cold and high elevations that it cannot survive in the lowlands.

Tibetans have domesticated the yak for use as a beast of burden. They also drink its milk and churn it to make butter. They eat its flesh and use its hide for making clothes and shelters. The dung is burned for fuel.

◀ Vicuñas ▲ Yak

6

Fresh Waters

Alligator

The American alligator *(Alligator mississipiensis)* is the largest reptile in North America. Two hundred years ago, alligators measuring as much as twenty feet long (6.1 m) inhabited the swamps and waterways of the southern United States. Over the years they were reduced almost to extinction. Many were slaughtered for their hides and for meat; others were killed to eliminate them as dangerous beasts near habitations. Young alligators were captured and sold to tourists as pets (never good ones, incidentally, and dangerous if they survived long enough to become sizable). In addition, much of their habitat was destroyed. Given protection by laws, the alligator has made an incredible comeback and is now plentiful again in many areas of Florida and elsewhere in the South.

The American alligator's nearest relative is the Chinese alligator *(Alligator sinensis),* which lives in the Yangtze River. The Chinese alligator is said to have inspired the Chinese dragon motif.

Alligators spend much of their time in the water, emerging to bask in the sun. In the water they can float with only their eyes and nostrils above the surface. Both are on bulbous protuberances. When they submerge, their nostrils are tightly closed with valves, as are their ear openings. Their jaws shut

◀ Lake, New Jersey

with a lidlike overlap so that no water gets inside their mouth, and their eyes are protected with a transparent third eyelid, or nictitating membrane. On land an alligator normally crawls slowly on its belly, but if it is disturbed, it will stand on its legs and run very rapidly for short distances. Its long flat tail is its principal source of power for swimming and is also a formidable weapon. The alligator's jaws, studded with sharp conical teeth, shut with such great force and so securely that an animal that tries to escape will have its limbs torn from its body. Oddly, however, the muscles for opening the jaws are so weak that a person can hold the jaws shut with one hand.

In spring, male alligators bellow like bulls to proclaim tenancy of a territory. Their loud roars may carry for a mile or more over swampy lowlands, and nearby, the earth trembles from the sound. Female alligators lay their eggs in mounds of mud and vegetation pushed together with their snout. The mound may be as much as three feet high (91.4 cm) and twice as wide at the base. The eggs—five to six dozen—are laid in a hollow dug in the center of the mound and then covered with debris. Each egg is nearly twice the size of a chicken egg, its shell leathery or rubbery. The heat from the decaying debris incubates the eggs, but the female stays nearby for the two months or longer that it takes for them to hatch. The young alligators cut their way from the shells with an eggtooth on top of their snout. They dig their way out of the nest and are

▲ Alligator

immediately on their own, getting no aid or protection from their mother.

Fifteen feet (4.5 m) is exceptionally large for an alligator today. All of the similar and closely related caimans *(Caiman sp.)* of South America are smaller. The giants among today's crocodilians are the slim-snouted gavials *(Gavialis gangeticus)* that live in the rivers and brackish waters of southeastern Asia. The record length for a gavial is twenty-one feet (6.4 m). The true crocodiles *(Crocodylus sp.)*, some inhabiting salt water, are mostly smaller, but several species attain lengths of about fifteen feet. The American crocodile *(Crocodylus acutus)*, with record lengths to over twenty feet but usually about half as long, is distinguished from the American alligator by its narrower snout and by the exposure of the fourth tooth in the lower jaw on each side when the jaws are shut. In the alligator, this tooth is hidden.

Alligator Gar

Gars *(Lepisosteus sp.)* are primitive freshwater fish, once widely distributed in the world but now confined to the Mississippi River and its tributaries in North America and to Central America and Cuba. A gar's air bladder is richly supplied with blood vessels and can be used as a "lung," permitting these fish to survive in even stagnant waters by coming to the surface from time to time to take in gulps of air. Gars have a slim, cigar-shaped body, their mouth projected into a slim, tooth-studded snout. Their dorsal and anal fins are located far to the rear, almost at the tail, and their scales, which are made of an extremely hard substance called ganoin, do not overlap but fit one against the other like bricks in a wall. Because of their hardness, the scales of large gars were used by the Indians to tip their arrows and spears, and pioneers wrapped their wooden plowshares with garhide.

The alligator gar *(Lepisosteus spatula)* is the giant of its clan and also one of the largest freshwater fishes in North America. It may reach a weight of three hundred pounds (136 kg) and measure ten feet (3 m) in length. Literature indicates that individuals twice this size were killed in the past, but these reports may have been exaggerated. Six-foot (1.8-m) alligator

gars are actually considered large today. The alligator gar has a relatively short, broad snout, much like an alligator's. It lives only in streams along the Gulf of Mexico in the southeastern United States.

Alligator Snapping Turtle

Largest of all North American turtles, the alligator snapper *(Macroclemys temmincki)* may exceed two hundred pounds (90.7 kg) in weight. This ugly giant lives in rivers tributary to the Gulf of Mexico in the extreme southeastern United States. Its sharp horny jaws are powerful enough to snip wires in two, to cut through sticks the size of broom handles, or even to sever a man's arm. Fortunately, the alligator snapper is not aggressive unless molested. It has even developed a lethargic but highly effective means of procuring food. Resting on the bottom, the big turtle opens its mouth wide, causing a pinkish wormlike filament on its tongue to become distended. This strange appendage wiggles in the slightest current, looking deceptively and enticingly like a worm. If a fish makes the mistake of swimming inside the jaws to get this tidbit, the giant simply lets its mouth fall shut, and it has its meal.

Anaconda

Whether this giant water-loving boa of the American tropics or the reticulated python *(Python reticulatus)* of southeastern Asia is the largest snake in the world has long been debated.

▲ Alligator snapping turtle

Records of reticulated pythons nearly thirty feet long (9 m) and weighing more than 250 pounds (113.4 kg) have been substantiated, and there was also a reported kill of a thirty-two-foot (9.8-m) python. Authenticated reports for the anaconda *(Eunectes murinus)*, a much heavier snake, are twenty-five feet (7.6 m) in length and a weight of about five hundred pounds (226.8 kg). Natives of the tropics have always insisted that much larger anacondas still live in the wilds, and a few years ago an engineering party in Colombia killed and measured a 37½-foot (11.4-m) snake, their record now accepted by many authorities. The snake was not weighed, but it is estimated that a thousand pounds (453.6 kg) would not be excessive for an anaconda this size.

The anaconda lives in northern South America and is always found along rivers, which it enters frequently. It preys on birds and mammals of almost any size that come to the river, commonly dropping on them from branches overhead. Like other members of the boa family, the anaconda kills by constricting, swallowing its prey head-first as soon as its powerful muscles have caused the animal's death by suffocation.

The anaconda's close relative, the boa constrictor *(Constrictor constrictor)*, is the best known of the giant snakes, its maximum recorded length eighteen feet (5.5 m) but few exceeding ten feet (3 m). Also found in the American tropics and subtropics, the boa constrictor is thought of as strictly a forest dweller but ranges through grasslands and even into deserts.

▲ Anaconda

Anhinga

Close relatives of cormorants, the anhingas *(Anhinga anhinga)* have exceptionally long necks and straight, sharp bills. Snakebird, darter, and water turkey are other names for the anhinga. Often the anhinga swims with only its head and neck above the surface. When fishing, it holds its neck in an S shape close to its body and then lashes out or strikes like a snake when it comes close to a fish. The anhinga actually spears its catches, the only bird to do so. At the surface, the anhinga flicks its bill and tosses the fish into the air, then catches it again in its opened bill, juggling it into position for swallowing head-first. Lacking a water-resistant coating of oil on its flight feathers, the anhinga follows each fishing foray by climbing into trees or shrubs at the water's edge and spreading its wings to dry.

Four species of anhingas occur in warm to tropical regions of the world, inhabiting streams, lakes, ponds, and occasionally brackish water.

Arapaima *(pronounced Ar-a-pie-ma)*
One of the largest of all freshwater fishes, the arapaima *(Arapaima gigas)* commonly reaches a length of eight feet (2.4 m) and a weight of two hundred pounds (90.7 kg). There are unauthenticated reports of arapaimas twice as large. These big-eyed fish, which live in large streams in northern South America, have long dorsal and anal fins that are almost continuous with the tail or caudal fin. Like other primitive fish, their air bladder is well supplied with blood vessels and is connected directly to the mouth cavity so that it serves as a "lung" for breathing air.

Archerfish
The six-inch (15.2-cm) archerfish *(Toxotes jaculatrix)* of southeastern Asia inhabits swamps and rivers, both brackish and freshwater. It cruises near the surface looking for spiders or insects in the overhanging branches of trees and shrubs, and when it spies a potential meal, it knocks it from its perch with well-aimed drops of water. An archerfish can spit accurately at distances up to four feet (1.2 m). It takes careful aim before firing, moving back and forth in the water to adjust its position before letting loose its pellets of water. Because of this peculiar habit, archerfish are often exhibited in aquariums. At one aquarium, the fish persisted in shooting out the lights over its tank until the bulbs were shielded.

◀ Anhinga ▲ Arapaima

Bitterling

A social parasite, like the cuckoos and the cowbird in the bird world, the three-inch (7.6-cm) female bitterling *(Rhodeus sericeus)* develops an ovipositor almost as long as her body. She inserts this ovipositor into a clam's shell and lays her eggs in its mantle cavity. The male bitterling spreads his milt in front of the clam's siphons, and the sperm are drawn inside with the currents of water in the clam's normal feeding and respiration processes. The bitterling's eggs hatch inside the mantle cavity, and the hatchlings spend several days there before setting off on their own. Members of the minnow family, bitterlings are natives of Europe.

Blind Salamander

Cave-dwelling salamanders and others that inhabit artesian wells hundreds of feet deep are among the more curious amphibians. Adults are colorless and blind, and because food is lacking in the deep waters, some of these salamanders must get their nutrition directly from the water by osmosis through their skin.

Candiru

No more than two inches long (5 cm), the South American candiru *(Vandellia cirrhosa)* is one of the smallest of all the catfishes. It can also be the most treacherous. Semiparasitic, this little fish swims inside the mouth cavity, gill chambers, or urogenital opening of its host victim and anchors itself securely in place by lifting its spined gill covers. Then it chews at

Archerfish ▲ Blind salamander ▶

the victim's tissues and feeds on the blood. The candiru does not exclude humans, and those who go into the water naked are potential prey. Once anchored, a candiru can be removed only by surgery unless it decides to unhook itself.

Climbing Perch

Known also as the walking fish, the ten-inch (25.4-cm) climbing perch *(Anabas testudineus)* lives in the swamps of southeastern Asia. Using its pectoral fins as legs, it walks over mud flats, and like the walking catfish, it may travel for long distances overland to find a new "home" if the pool in which it has been living dries up. Over its gills is a labyrinth of chambers richly supplied with blood vessels and serving as a "lung" for breathing air, enabling the climbing perch to remain out of water for as long as these chambers stay moist. Bettas *(Betta splendens)* and gouramis *(Osphronemus goramy)*, popular aquarium fishes, are close relatives of the climbing perch.

Congo Eel

Largest of the amphibians in the United States, one species attaining a length of three and a half feet (1 m), congo eels *(Amphiuma means)* live in ditches, swamps, and sluggish streams throughout the Southeast. They have four legs, but they are dwarfed and useless. Their body is slim, slippery, and quite eellike. These strange salamanders are quick to bite, and they hold on firmly while twisting their body, which may tear chunks from their victim.

Cormorant

Like loons and grebes, the long-necked cormorants *(Phalacrocorax sp.)* lack large air sacs in their body to make them buoyant. With their specific gravity nearly equal to that of water, they need only expel some air from their lungs or release whatever air may be trapped under their wings or in their feathers in order to sink. Cormorants are expert fishermen, making their catches while swimming underwater but almost always coming to the surface to juggle the fish into position before swallowing it. Some thirty species of cormorants occur in coastal and nearby inland waters around the world.

In the Orient, the cormorant's prowess at catching fish was exploited commercially for centuries. Tethered and wearing a metal ring or thong around the base of its long neck, the "working" bird was turned loose in the water among schools of fish to make its catches. As soon as its throat was stuffed, the bird was pulled back to the boat, where a fisherman would strip out the fish and then let the bird resume its work. Each bird would be given at least one throatful of fish as a reward.

▲ Cormorants

Electric Eel

A full-grown electric eel *(Electrophorus electricus)* may be eight feet long (2.4 m), with roughly half of its body weight in the highly specialized muscles that produce electricity. This electrical generator located in the tail can produce a jolt of six hundred volts. The eel uses its electricity not only to knock out prey but also, when released in short pulses, for navigational signals similar to but much less sophisticated than the echolocation system of bats. The echoed electrical pulses are recorded by special receiving structures on the eel's head. A young eel has excellent vision, but in older eels, the eyes become nearly useless while the strength of the electrical generators becomes greater. Electric eels do not have either dorsal or ventral fins, but the anal fin stretches the full length of the body and supplies the power for swimming. These unusual eels live in the streams of tropical and subtropical South America.

Four-eyed Fish

A native of Mexico and Central America, where it lives in muddy streams, the four-eyed fish *(Anableps anableps)* has bulbous, froglike eyes on top of its head. The fish swims at the surface, its eyes half in and half out of the water. Each eye is

▲ Electric eel

actually divided into two lobes so that it functions as two eyes, one for seeing in the air and the other for seeing in the water. The lens in each eye is egg-shaped rather than spherical. In the water, light passes through the entire length of the lens; in the air, only through its shorter width. Thus, when looking in the water, the four-eyed fish is nearsighted, which is typical of fishes, but in the air it has good distance vision for seeing insects or other prey. The retina at the back of the eye is divided so that the two different kinds of images are recorded separately.

Four-eyed fish are peculiar also in having sex organs that are turned either to the right or to the left. A "left" male can mate only with a "right" female, and vice versa.

Freshwater Eel

The freshwater eels of Europe and America journey to the sea to lay their eggs, the details of their strange spawning trip not known until a Danish scientist solved the mystery in the late 1800s. Until then it was not known where eels originated. Many believed they came from horsehairs that somehow sprang into life. The real story is almost as unbelievable.

Both the American *(Anguilla rostrata)* and European *(Anguilla anguilla)* eels travel through the Atlantic to an area at the edge of the Sargasso Sea—a trip of about a thousand miles (1,609 km) through the sea for the American eels and three thousand miles (4,827 km) for the European. Here each female lays literally millions of eggs. A large female, for example, can produce twenty million eggs. The males release their milt over

Four-eyed fish ▲ Freshwater eels ▶

the eggs, and then both adults disappear, dying somewhere at sea.

Leaf-thin and transparent, the young or glass eels that hatch from the eggs are at first not even recognizable as eels. They drift with the currents as a part of the plankton, swimming only enough to keep themselves directed toward their "homes," each kind knowing by some mysterious directional force which way to go—the American eels moving westward, the European eels eastward. American eels complete their journey in about a year; for the baby European eels, the trip requires three years. Amazingly, their rates of development are different so that they are about the same size when they arrive at the freshwater streams up which they travel to spend their adult lives. By this time, in fact, they look very much like diminutive adults, and they are called elvers.

Young males typically stay near the mouths of streams, close to the sea. The females continue their journey to the headwaters, or they may squirm snakelike through wet or dewy grass to get into ponds or lakes with no direct connection to streams. Some of these landlocked eels never go back to the sea to spawn. A full-grown female eel is about three feet long (91.4 cm), the males only about a foot long. After several years, the females begin to move downstream on their way to the Sargasso Sea. As they pass through the mouths of rivers, they are joined by males, then head out to sea to spawn and to die.

Giant Salamander

The world's largest living amphibian, the giant salamander *(Megalobatrachus japonicus)* reaches a length of five feet (1.5 m). Inhabiting Japan and China, it moves sluggishly along pool bottoms, spending much of its time resting. This big salamander is caught and sold in markets for food.

The North American hellbender *(Cryptobranchus alleghaniensis),* a foot and a half long (45.7 cm), is a member of the same family. The hellbender lives in the Ohio River and its tributary streams, west to the Mississippi and south to Georgia and Louisiana.

Grebe

A grebe *(Podiceps sp.)* usually floats high in the water, but it has the unusual ability to expel air from its body so that it can sink out of sight quickly, going down like a submarine. It can swim while nearly submerged, keeping only its eyes and its bill above the surface. Grebe chicks ride on their mother's back, often hidden under her wings. If she dives, they bob to the surface like corks. Grebes also have the strange habit of eating their own feathers.

The eighteen species of small ducklike grebes are found throughout the world in temperate and cool climates. They favor freshwater streams, lakes, and ponds, but may also occur in coastal areas. Several species are found only in the Andes at elevations of more than ten thousand feet (3,048 m).

Hairy Frog

The most bizarre of all frogs is the male hairy frog *(Astylosternus robustus)* that lives in the Cameroons in western Africa. During the breeding season, it grows a beard-thick fringe of hairlike filaments along its sides and thighs. This is apparently not simply decorative, like the plumes developed by many cock birds; it provides a greater exposure of surface area for respiration through the skin. This supplies the male with the additional oxygen needed in his sexual performances.

Hillstream Fish

 These three- to four-inch (7.6–10.2-cm) minnowlike fish *(Gas-*

Hippopotamus ▶

tromyzon sp.) live in swift streams in the hilly regions of southeastern Asia. The bases of their fins are joined to form a suction device that helps them to hold on in currents. Clingfishes, a family of small marine fishes (Gobieoscidae) found in warm seas throughout the world, have fins similarly adapted for holding on in moving water.

Hippopotamus

These African giants are exceeded in size only by elephants. They average one and a half to two tons in weight (1,361–1,814.4 kg), but some males may weigh as much as four tons. Hippos *(Hippopotamus amphibius)* spend most of their time nearly submerged in streams or lakes. Young hippos are born

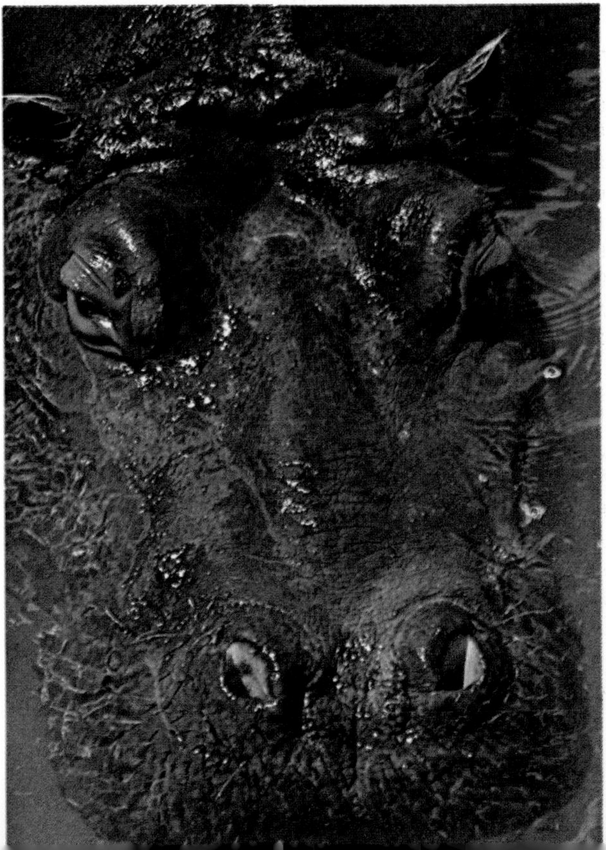

underwater and even nurse underwater. They can swim before they can walk. Hippos may wander inland at night to browse, but they are best adapted for their watery habitat.

A hippo's eyes are set on bulbous protuberances on its enormous head, enabling the animal to submerge all except its eyes and still see. Keeping underwater is a protection from flies and other insects. The hippo's nostrils, mere slits at the top of the flat muzzle, close tightly when the animal submerges. Compared to the size of its head, a hippo's ears are tiny, but the mouth is cavernous, the lower canines tusklike and the incisors sticking out almost at right angles. A hippo's yawn is a purposeful display of this weaponry.

Though cumbersome on land, a hippo moves with ease in the water, which buoys its massive body. On its short, stout legs it can walk or even run along the bottom, completely out of sight except for the trail of mud rising to the surface. It can remain underwater for nearly half an hour before having to surface for air. A hippo can also float, its usual position for sleeping. Some tales credit hippos with sweating blood, but they do not. In the heat of the sun or when excited, however, they do excrete a reddish, foul-smelling oily fluid.

Leaffish

Leaffish are protectively shaped and colored, looking almost identical to a leaf that has fallen into the water. Their stubby chin barbel resembles the stem of the leaf. This camouflage

permits the leaffish to get close to its prey without being noticed. A native of South America, the four-inch (10.2-cm) leaffish *(Monocirrhus polyacanthus)* is commonly kept in aquariums. It is the only member of its family with this sort of deceptive shape and pattern.

Loon

Some people describe the call of the loon as weird or even maniacal; others rate it as one of nature's symphonic treats. No one denies that the cry of the loon is hauntingly melancholy.

The four species of loons *(Gavia sp.)* are natives of northern regions. They usually nest along freshwater lakes or ponds and winter in coastal seas. Though their wings are small, loons are expert fliers. They take off by running across the surface of the water, and once airborne they may reach speeds of sixty miles per hour (96.5 km/hr). Some migrate for a thousand or more miles from polar nesting grounds to warmer winter quarters.

While most birds have hollow or spongy bones, loons' bones are solid, making the birds heavy. A loon's specific gravity is so close to that of water that it can easily sink below the surface simply by letting the air out of its lungs. This enables it literally to drop out of sight without making a commotion on the surface. A loon's legs are encased in its body all the way to the ankles; and its feet are webbed. As a result, it moves clumsily and is uncomfortable on land, but swims and dives expertly. It can dive to depths of two hundred feet or more (61 m) and may remain submerged for as long as five minutes.

◀ Leaffish ▲ Loon

Lungfish

Considered the most ancient of living fishes until the discovery of the coelacanth (which see), the lungfishes of South America, Australia, and Africa trace their ancestry directly to types that lived 300 million years ago. Their air bladder, which serves other fishes as a hydrostatic organ in regulating their specific gravity for various depths in the water, has been modified to function as a lung. It is richly supplied with blood vessels and is connected directly to the mouth so that the fish can use it for breathing air. In fact, a lungfish will drown unless it surfaces regularly to take in gulps of air. The exception is the Australian lungfish *(Neoceratodus forsteri),* which has both lungs and gills and can breathe equally well in either air or water. The Australian lungfish may reach a length of five feet (1.5 m) and weigh twenty pounds (9 kg). South American lungfish *(Lepidosiren paradoxa),* to four feet long (1.2 m), also have gills, but they are apparently little used.

The best known lungfishes are the four African species *(Protopterus sp.),* their fins reduced to cordlike filaments. Like the other lungfishes, they inhabit wetlands and swamps that dry up at one season of the year. When this happens, the lungfish squirm into the mud at the bottom of the drying pool and secrete around themselves a cocoon of mucus that is connected to the surface by a vent for breathing. The mud

Lungfish ▲

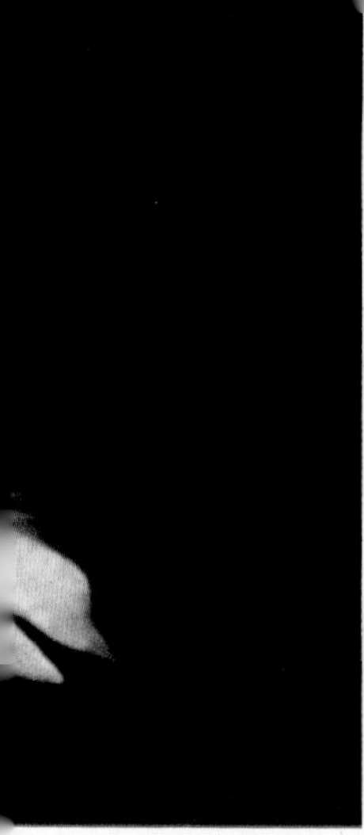

bakes hard in the sun, but the fish survives in its moist enclosure. When rains come again and soften the mud, the fish emerge and resume their usual activity. Their "cocoons" are dug up with the fish inside and shipped around the world. Lungfish have been known to live for several years in these cocoons, taking no food and losing half or more of their weight during the period of dormancy.

Matamata

Of all turtles, the matamata *(Chelys fimbriata)* is the ugliest. On its carapace are three rows of triangular bumps, and the skin on its snakelike neck, longer than its carapace, is flabby and warty. Its head is triangular, the snout flattened into a snorkel-like proboscis. This strange sixteen-inch (40.6-cm) turtle that lives in the rivers of northern South America is unusual, too, in having very weak jaws. Hidden in debris on the river bottom, the matamata waits for a fish to swim close, then opens its huge mouth and lets the water rush in. If the matamata has judged the distance well, its meal is swept in with the current, and the turtle simply shuts its mouth and swallows the fish whole. The fringes of skin on its neck apparently help to attract prey. The matamata cannot withdraw its neck into its shell. Instead it turns its head and neck sideways, managing only to get its tender nose tucked out of sight and reach.

Matamata ▲

▲ Mormyrids ▼ Oystercatchers ▲ Paddlefish

Mormyrid *(pronounced More-my-rid)*
About a hundred species of these unusual freshwater fishes *(Mormyrus sp., Gnathonemus sp.,* and others) live in tropical Africa. Nearly all have a peculiarly projected mouth that resembles an elephant's trunk. Some reach a length of five feet (1.5 m), but most are only about six inches long (15.2 cm). Mormyrids can generate electricity, the weak shocks apparently an aid in helping them locate food rather than a protective device or a weapon to kill or stun prey. The muscles generating the electricity are located near the base of the tail.

Nutria
Nutrias *(Myocastor coypus)* are unusual, three-and-a-half-foot, twenty-pound (1-m, 9-kg) South American rodents that bear a remarkable resemblance to the shmoos in Al Capp's comic strip "Li'l Abner." They have webbed hind feet like a duck, handlike front paws similar to a monkey's, the long and

bristly whiskers of a walrus, the sleek body of an otter, the chisel-sharp teeth of a beaver, and the round handlelike tail of a muskrat. The female's mammary glands are located along her sides rather than on her belly, enabling a mother to suckle her young while she swims and forages. In young animals, the huge incisors are bright orange; in mature animals, mahogany-red.

Natives of temperate regions of South America, nutrias were introduced to Europe in 1929 and to the United States in 1930. At first kept in cages as curiosities in Louisiana, some escaped in 1939 by digging themselves out, and the following year many more got out when a hurricane wrecked their pens. Within a few years the prolific nutrias—females may have two or more broods per year—had populated the Louisiana swamps and were spreading northward. In Louisiana they are now a major fur resource, having pushed out the native muskrats in most areas. Most properly, in fact, the name nutria refers only to the fur; the animal's correct name is coypu.

Oystercatcher

An oystercatcher's *(Haematopus sp.)* bill is more than twice as long as the bird's head and is flattened vertically so that it is knifelike. The tip is blunt. With this powerful instrument, an oystercatcher can open clam or oyster shells; the bill may also be used for probing in the mud. Six species are generally recognized, ranging widely along the coasts of Europe, Africa, and North America.

Paddlefish

Also called spoonbill, the now-rare paddlefish *(Polyodon spathula)* is a primitive fish closely related to sturgeons. There are two species, one found in the Mississippi River and its tributaries and the other in the Yangtze River in China, a distribution paralleling the alligator's. The paddlefish's flat, spoonlike snout may be half as long as its body. This sensitive paddle is used in searching for food in the mud. The fish lacks scales except for a few patches near the tail. The paddlefish may reach a length of six feet (1.8 m) and weigh as much as 180 pounds (81.6 kg).

Piranha *(pronounced Pi-ran-ya)*

Piranhas *(Serrasalmus sp.)* are considered to be the most voracious and vicious of all fishes. They have a mouth full of razor-sharp teeth and will bite anything that moves. Blood or a commotion in the water attracts large numbers of piranhas to the scene and sends them into a frenzy. Within minutes the bloodthirsty little fish can chop up and consume an animal the size of a cow or a pig. In the foray, some of the piranhas become victims themselves. Ordinarily piranhas make their meals of smaller animals, of course, and the tales told about them become more exaggerated with each telling. They are nevertheless not the kind of fish to be kept in home aquariums, and laws in the United States now prohibit their sale or importation because of the danger to the people who keep them and because of the threat they would pose if they escaped and became established in the warm waters of the South.

Piranhas are natives of freshwater streams in northern South America. Many of the roughly five hundred species that belong to the same family as piranhas are popular with fish hobbyists. As a group, they are known as the characins. Most members of the family are from the tropics and subtropics of Central and South America; a few are native to Africa. One of the most interesting is the blind cave fish from Mexico. It is a favorite with hobbyists because of the ease with which it moves through an aquarium without bumping into objects even though it cannot see.

Red piranha ▲ Snowy plover ▶

Plover

Plovers are shore birds, dozens of species ranging from small to medium in size found throughout the world. A few, such as the familiar killdeer *(Charadrius vociferus)* in North America, inhabit uplands. Several have developed unusual feeding habits and adaptations. New Zealand's crooked-billed plover or wrybill *(Anarhynchus frontalis)* has a curiously twisted bill, the terminal quarter bent to the right. The crooked-billed plover feeds on insects and other small animals found along beaches, its bent bill apparently useful in extracting these creatures from beneath rocks or other objects. The crocodile bird *(Hoplopterus spinosus),* found in Africa and southeastern Asia, reportedly has the unusual habit of walking into a crocodile's gaped mouth to pick off leeches. It also has sharp spurs at the bend of its wings for use as weapons in fighting. The Egyptian plover *(Pluvianus aegyptius)* also goes by the name of crocodile bird and is said to have the same daring habit of entering crocodiles' mouths. The Egyptian plover, which is actually a courser rather than a true plover, lays its eggs in the sand and then sits over them to shield them from the sun. The female makes regular trips to get water to wet her breast feathers and then to moisten the eggs and the sand around them.

Skimmer

A skimmer's lower bill is almost 50 percent longer than the upper bill, unique among all birds, and it is flattened to knife thinness vertically. Interestingly, when a skimmer first hatches, the halves of its bill are the same length; the differences in length do not become pronounced until the bird is nearly full-grown.

An adult skimmer flies so close to the water that its lower bill slices the surface. When it strikes a fish or a shrimp, the upper half closes quickly to convert the hapless victim into a meal. The edges of the bills are sharp for holding the prey firmly, and the skimmer's neck muscles are extraordinarily large to cushion the shock of striking objects. Because it flies so close to the surface, a skimmer's wings do not go below the level of its body on the downstroke.

There are three species of skimmers in the world: the black skimmer *(Rynchops nigra)*, which ranges along the Atlantic coasts of North and South America; the Indian skimmer *(Rynchops albicollis)*, occurring in India and nearby countries of southern Asia; and the African skimmer *(Rynchops flavirostris)*, found along the coasts as well as inland in Africa.

Sturgeon

Armored with bony plates, a sturgeon *(Acipenser sp., Scaphirhynchus sp.,* and others) looks like a creature from the geologic past. Indeed, sturgeons are "living fossils," only a few dozen species existing today but abundantly represented by fossils. Some sturgeons inhabit fresh waters exclusively; others live in the sea but move into fresh waters to spawn. Sturgeons are long-lived, some of them estimated to exceed 150 years in age. All have a flattened shovellike snout with sensory barbels hanging down near the tip. When these sense food on the bottom, the tubelike mouth, located a few inches behind the barbels, is protruded to pick up the morsels.

Sturgeons have been harvested heavily as food fish, particularly for their roe, the favored caviar of Europe. A large female may produce 250 to 300 pounds of roe, totaling some three million eggs. Unauthenticated reports from Russia tell of belugas *(Huso huso),* which are sturgeons, weighing one and a half tons (1,360 kg) and almost thirty feet long (9 m). In the early 1800s, many white sturgeons *(Acipenser transmontanus)* weighing more than a thousand pounds (453.6 kg) were caught in the Pacific Northwest, mainly in the Columbia and Fraser rivers. Several weighing more than fifteen hundred pounds (680.4 kg) were also reported. Sturgeons are unquestionably the largest of all freshwater fishes.

Surinam Toad

Its flat body almost square and its head triangular, with small beadlike eyes, the Surinam toad *(Pipa pipa)* is one of the most freakish of all amphibians. It lives in muddy streams in north-

◀ Black skimmer ▲ Russian sturgeon (beluga)

ern South America and rarely leaves the water. The toes on its front legs end in star-shaped discs, and its hind legs are broadly webbed. Unusual for frogs and toads, the Surinam toad does not have a tongue, which is used by its land-dwelling kin for capturing prey in the air but is useless in the water. It shares this lack with the clawed frog of Africa *(Xenopus laevis)*, a member of the same family and similar in habits and habitat.

The Surinam toad is strangest, however, in the way it cares for its eggs. As the female lays her eggs, the male spreads sperm over them and at the same time presses them one at a time into the soft skin on the female's back. Each egg occupies a separate pocket that becomes grown over with a "lid." In these containers, the eggs (as many as sixty in all) hatch and develop, emerging as diminutive toadlets. The female then rubs off the thick pad on her back, her procreative duties completed for the year.

Talking Catfish

These eight-inch (20.3-cm) freshwater catfish *(Acanthodoras spinosissimus)* of South America make their "talking" noises, which are grunting or croaking sounds, by changing the pressure in their air bladder and causing it to vibrate. They are especially noisy when caught and removed from the water.

Many kinds of marine fish make noises in a similar manner. Many of the sea catfish (which see) produce grunting, squeaking, growling, and even mewing sounds.

▲ Surinam toad

Upside-down Catfish

These popular three-inch (7.6-cm) catfish *(Synodontis nigriventris)* from tropical Africa spend most of their time swimming on their backs. When young, they swim in a normal position but spend increasingly longer times on their backs as they mature. An upside-down catfish's belly is darker than its back, the opposite of most fish and evidence that this reversed position has an ancient evolutionary history.

Weatherfish

When a weatherfish becomes very active, it is a sign that the barometer has dropped and that a storm is likely. As the barometer rises, a weatherfish becomes less active. The fish apparently registers changes in barometric pressure in its air bladder, which is divided into two compartments. The first, presumably the "weather" instrument, is encased in a bony capsule.

There are two species of weatherfish, one in Europe and the other in Asia. The European weatherfish *(Misgurnus fossilis)* may reach a length of eighteen inches (45.7 cm) but averages about eight inches (20.3 cm); the Asian or spined weatherfish *(Cobitis taenia)* averages four inches (10.2 cm). They belong to the loach family, many species of which are popular with fish hobbyists. Weatherfish, in fact, are kept in aquariums and watched with interest to check the accuracy of their prognostications.

▲ Upside-down catfish

7

Australia and Oceanic Islands

Aye-Aye

Aye-ayes *(Daubentonia madagascariensis)* live in the forests on the island of Madagascar. Cat-sized primitive primates related to lemurs and lorises, they have curiously long bony fingers and toes, the middle finger on each hand exceptionally long and tapered. This is used to tap branches to locate hollows or to cause a detectable stirring inside, indicating the presence of grubs. The finger is then employed like a hooked probe to pull out the morsel. It is useful also in picking insects from beneath bark and as a sort of spoon for digging out the insides of edible stems, such as sugar cane.

Babirusa *(pronounced Bab-a-roo-sa)*

One of the most grotesque of all mammals, the male babirusa *(Babyrousa babyrussa)* has outlandishly large tusks, or canines. The upper tusks grow out through the upper lip and then curve upward, sometimes almost making a complete circle. The lower tusks grow alongside them, their curve less exaggerated. No function can be ascribed to these extraordinary outgrowths except as secondary sexual characteristics. This is one of a number of examples in nature where the evolution of a structure has gone beyond usefulness. Babirusa, the local name for these pigs that live in the swampy forests of

◀ Raiatea Island, French Polynesia

the Celebes and on nearby islands, literally means "pig deer," presumably because the tusks resemble antlers. It is a native belief that babirusas hang by their tusks to sleep at night—not true, of course.

Bird of Paradise

Of all birds, no group surpasses the birds of paradise for fantastic beauty. During the breeding season, the males are riots of color, with unbelievably lavish plumage. As if aware of their striking handsomeness, they go through elaborate displays, lifting and spreading their feathers until they are almost unrecognizable as birds. In some species even the inside of the mouth is astonishingly colorful, and the birds gape to show off this startling splendor. More than forty species of birds of paradise live on New Guinea and nearby islands, some in lowland forests and others high in the mountains. Some are no bigger than sparrows, others the size of crows.

Bowerbird

About twenty species of bowerbirds inhabit the brush and forest lands of Australia and New Guinea. No birds make more elaborate areas for courtship. Built by the males, these bowers are used to attract the females. After mating, the females go off

Aye-aye ▲ Bird of paradise ▶

to build their own nests elsewhere, and the male does not participate.

The canopies under which the males court vary in size and complexity with the species. The golden bowerbird *(Prionodura newtoniana),* less than ten inches long (25.4 cm) itself, constructs a bower that is nearly ten feet tall (3 m), using a sapling tree as the center. Others make bowers that are not as tall but that consist of a number of compartments or rooms. Some color the walls of each room with a "paint" made of saliva mixed with charcoal or plant pigments, using leaves like brushes to apply the color. Bowerbirds typically decorate the floors of their bowers with freshly plucked flowers, ferns, feathers, bones, shells, berries, bark, stones, or other items. If a choice of color is possible, a bowerbird will select blue above all others. When bright objects become dull, they are replaced with new ones. Once it has built a bower, a male may occupy it for nearly a year.

Cassowary *(pronounced Cas-a-wer-rie)*

Living in the tropical forests of Australia, New Guinea, and on some nearby islands, cassowaries *(Casuarius sp.)* are large flightless birds that may stand more than five feet tall (1.5 m). On their head they wear a large bony helmet or casque, a protection when they run through the underbrush. The naked skin on the head is generally blue or purple, and bright red wattles hang from the throat. Unusual among birds, the females are larger than the males.

Cassowaries are wary and normally avoid confrontation with humans, but if cornered, they can be extremely dangerous, leaping into the air and making powerful slashes with their spike-sharp claws.

Echidna *(pronounced Ee-kid-na)*

Also called spiny anteaters, echidnas *(Tachyglossus aculeatus* and *Zaglossus bruijni)* are primitive egg-laying mammals that live in Australia, New Guinea, and Tasmania. The two species

Cassowary ▲ Echidna ▶

of echidnas and the platypus (which see) form a special order of mammals, the monotremes. The name refers to the single opening, called a cloaca, that is used both for the elimination of wastes and for reproduction. A female echidna lays one or, rarely, two rubbery-shelled eggs in a pouch on the underside of her abdomen. Here the egg hatches and the young develops, lapping up milk that is secreted directly into the pouch by the mammary glands. The female has no teats.

The echidna's body is covered with sharp barbless spines. For protection, it rolls into a ball and becomes an an untouchable thorny mass, or if there is time, it burrows into loose soil. An echidna has powerful claws and can dig with great speed. Males also have a poisonous spine on each hind leg. Echidnas feed on termites and ants, digging into their nests and then using their long, wormlike tongue to pick up the insects.

Flapfooted Lizard

These snakelike lizards of Australia, New Guinea, and nearby islands do not have front legs, and their hind legs are reduced to scaly flaps scarcely distinguishable from their body scales. Flapfooted lizards move along the ground like snakes. In fact, snakelizard is another name by which they are known. Like snakes, they lack movable eyelids. Jicar's lialis *(Lialis jicari)*, largest of the twenty species, is two and a half feet long (76 cm).

Frilled Lizard

This eight-inch (20.3-cm) agamid lizard *(Chlamydosaurus kingi)* has a slim whiplike tail nearly two feet long (61 cm), but its most unusual feature is the frill of skin that hangs in loose folds around its neck. If it is disturbed, the lizard stands up stiffly on its front feet, lifts its head, and opens its mouth wide. Suddenly it expands its neck frill into a stiff collar that may measure almost six inches across (15.2 cm). Should it run to escape, it runs bipedally.

▲ Frilled lizard ▼ Galapagos tortoise

The frilled lizard lives in Australia. It shares its unusual defense mechanism with the somewhat smaller bearded lizard *(Amphibolurus barbatus),* which spreads a collar of stiff bristle-tipped scales and also displays the bright orange lining of its mouth.

Frogmouth

During the day, a frogmouth *(Podargus strigoides),* so named because of its wide froglike mouth, sleeps stretched out lengthwise on a branch, its head lifted and its eyes closed. Its mottled plumage gives it near-perfect camouflage against the bark so that it looks like the stub of a branch. A dozen species of frogmouths inhabit Australia and nearby islands. They are related to nighthawks and other nocturnal birds that catch their insect food on the wing, but frogmouths are specialists at hunting on the ground, taking not only insects and other invertebrates but also animals as large as mice.

Galapagos Tortoise

Of the more than three dozen species of tortoises (turtles that live on land) found throughout the world, more than half have shells that are two to three feet long (61–91.4 cm). The largest *(Geochelone elephantopus),* with shells more than four feet long (1.2 m), live on the Galapagos Islands in the Pacific Ocean off the western coast of South America. Aldabra tortoises *(Geochelone gigantea)* of the Seychelles Islands in the

▲ Frogmouth

Indian Ocean are equally large. These giants weigh more than five hundred pounds (226.8 kg) and are exceeded in size among turtles only by the marine leatherback (which see). An Aldabra tortoise that died accidentally in 1918 had been kept in captivity since 1766, and since it was already mature when captured, its age at death was estimated to be at least 180.

In their adaptation to life on land, tortoises have developed clubbed feet and stout legs, elephantine in appearance. In nearly all tortoises, the shell is domed or highly arched, and though the shell cannot be closed as in box turtles (which see), the head and appendages are drawn inside and the legs are folded over the front so that only the heavily scaled and spiny portions are exposed at the front and the scaly soles of the feet at the rear.

When the Galapagos Islands were discovered, they were inhabited by innumerable giant tortoises, which proved to be good to eat. In the days of sailing vessels, with a peak when the whaling fleets worked the Pacific, there was no refrigeration on the ships. These big tortoises, however, could be placed on their backs in the holds and kept alive for weeks or even months, supplying the crews with fresh meat when needed. The tortoises were also harvested in large numbers to get their oil. As the islands became inhabited, man's domestic animals—dogs, cats, and goats—took a heavy toll of tortoise eggs and young tortoises. No one knows how many hundreds of thousands of giant tortoises were killed, but the estimates range as high as ten million. By the 1960s their once incredible numbers were reduced to a few thousand. They are now protected by law.

Kangaroo

Kangaroos are the largest of the marsupials and are symbolic of Australia. Of the several dozen kinds, the red and gray kangaroos *(Macropus rufus* and *Macropus canguru)* are the giants, both measuring more than six feet long (1.8 m) including the tail and weighing as much as two hundred pounds (90.7 kg). Much of a kangaroo's weight is concentrated in its thick tail and its powerful hind legs, with which it can make horizontal jumps of twenty-five feet or more (7.6 m) and can

Red kangaroo ▶

clear fences to ten feet high. In its jumps, the kangaroo uses its tail as a balancer; at rest, it uses it as a prop, making a tripod with its legs. When fighting, in fact, a kangaroo can sit on its tail alone and at the same time kick with its hind feet. A kick from the powerful legs can be lethal. The small front legs are used in picking up food and also for boxing-type blows in both fight and play. A kangaroo can run about twenty miles per hour (32.2 km/hr) but may speed to twice as fast for short distances.

At birth a kangaroo is no bigger than a honeybee and is still embryonic. It completes its development in the mother's pouch, where it rides for six months or longer, even after it is able to move independently. Young kangaroos are called joeys.

The kangaroo clan includes many smaller varieties. Among them are the wallabies, wallaroos, tree kangaroos, and little rat kangaroos that are no more than a foot long (30.5 cm).

Kiwi

The chicken-sized kiwi *(Apteryx sp.)* holds the record in the bird world for laying the largest egg in proportion to the female's size—a four-pound (1.8-kg) hen produces an egg that weighs nearly a pound (453.6 g), a quarter of her own weight. The male incubates the egg in a moss-lined nest in a burrow.

Kiwis are flightless, and when they run, they wobble comically because of their short, widely spaced legs. Their wings are only about two inches long (5 cm). A kiwi's body feathers are long and coarse, looking like unkempt hair, and its bill is long and slim. Most unusual, the nostrils are at the tip of the bill; unlike most other birds, the kiwi has a keen sense of smell for finding the worms, grubs, and other animals on which it feeds. Bristles at the base of the bill are sensory. The eyes are small.

Kiwis—their name describes their strange call—are active only at night. The three similar species all live in New Zealand. They were once hunted heavily for food but are now protected.

Koala

A koala *(Phascolarctos cinereus)* looks like a teddy bear, and early settlers in Australia did, in fact, believe they were a kind of bear. Actually the koala is a marsupial, belonging to the same order as opossums and kangaroos. Once hunted exten-

sively for its fur and caught in large numbers for exhibit, it is now protected by law and has been provided with special sanctuaries.

Koalas eat only the leaves and flowers of particular kinds of eucalyptus or gum trees that are native to Australia, their fur and flesh acquiring a distinctively sweet odor from this highly specialized diet. Only a few zoos in the world are located where eucalyptus trees can be grown in sufficient abundance to keep koalas supplied with food.

In most marsupials the pouch opens at the top or to the front, but in koalas the pouch opens to the rear. This is not only unusual but also can be dangerous for the young since the mother spends most of her life climbing. Some of the ground-dwelling marsupials, such as the Tasmanian devil, also have pouches that open to the rear.

In the language of the aborigines, koala means "no drink," for these animals almost never drink water, getting all the moisture they need from the leaves and flowers they eat. Another strange feature of the koala is the exceptional length of its appendix—it can be as long as eight feet (2.4 m). This is related to its exclusively vegetarian diet, the appendix aiding in the digestion of the leaves.

◀ Kiwi ▲ Koala and young

Komodo Dragon

Ten feet long (3 m) and weighing as much as three hundred pounds (136 kg), the now-rare Komodo dragon *(Varanus komodoensis)* is the largest of all living lizards. This giant, big enough indeed to merit its dragon name, makes its meals of the small deer and pigs that inhabit the Indonesian island of Komodo. The lizards have been reduced to near extinction, partly because large numbers have been killed over the years but also because of scarcity of food. Even after the lizards were given protection their numbers continued to decline, for the laws did not prohibit hunters from killing the pigs and deer on which the lizards depend.

The Komodo dragon is a monitor lizard, a primarily tropical family in which there is great diversity in size. One Australian species is less than ten inches long (25.4 cm), but more than a dozen of the monitors are three to six feet long (91.4 cm–1.8 m). The Nile monitors are the largest reptiles in Africa next to the crocodiles, some of them exceeding eight feet in length (2.4 m).

Kookaburra *(pronounced Kook-a-boor-a)*

The kookaburra or "laughing jackass" *(Dacelo novaeguineae)* is an Australian forest-dwelling kingfisher and the largest of the kingfisher family, measuring about a foot and a half long (45.7 cm), or the size of a common crow. It is best known for its

Komodo dragon ▲ Kookaburra ▶

maniacal laughing cries, recordings of which are often used as background music in films about the tropics. In the wild, a kookaburra is noisiest just before going to roost at night and when it awakens in the morning. The kookaburra is famed, too, for killing snakes, but it will eat any small animal that it can catch.

Lyrebird

The male superb lyrebird *(Menura superba),* which lives in the forests of eastern Australia, has the most spectacular tail of all birds. The curved outer feathers, to two feet long (61 cm), form a frame in the shape of a lyre, and the delicate inner feathers look like the strings. Performing from atop a mound of dirt that he has scraped together, the male spreads this magnificent appendage, bending it forward over his body, during courtship displays.

Lyrebirds, particularly the males, are marvelous mimics, imitating the calls not only of other birds but also of other animals. They can also make sounds remarkably like train whistles, automobile horns, buzz saws—their repertoire includes virtually every noise they hear.

Marine Iguana

Five feet long (1.5 m) and weighing more than twenty pounds (9 kg), the marine iguana *(Amblyrhynchus cristatus)* inhabits the Galapagos Islands, where it lives among the rocks along the shore and dives into the sea to graze on sea lettuce and other seaweeds. This is the only lizard that depends on the sea for its meals.

The closely related and ill-tempered land iguana *(Conolophus subcristatus)* that also lives on the Galapagos Islands is one-third smaller. It inhabits the dry interior and feeds on the harsh plants that grow there, eating cacti, spines and all.

Moloch *(pronounced Moe-lock)*

The ugliest of all lizards, the Australian moloch's body *(Moloch horridus)* is completely covered with spines, those on the head especially large and arising from knoblike protuberances. Despite its formidable appearance, the moloch is harmless. Its diet consists wholly of ants, and it may lap up a thousand or more at a meal. Another name for the moloch is thorny devil.

Pandaka

Pandakas *(Pandaka pygmaea)* are tiny gobies that live in freshwater lakes in the Philippines. In length, they are the smallest of all vertebrates, measuring less than a half-inch (1.3 cm) when full-grown. They are harvested commercially in

Marine iguana ▲ Platypus ▶

fine-meshed nets and sold in markets for making fish cakes. It takes approximately fifteen thousand panadakas to weigh a pound.

Platypus

The platypus *(Ornithorhynchus anatinus)* is a mammal that lays eggs. Native to Australia and Tasmania, it inhabits streams and lakes, ranging to elevations of more than five thousand feet (1,524 m). About eighteen inches long (45.7 cm), the platypus has webbed feet, a flat ducklike bill covered with leathery skin, and a tail much like a beaver's. During the day it hides in burrows dug in banks along waterways, coming out at night to feed on crayfish, worms, and other small animals that it finds by grubbing in the mud or sand with its sensitive bill. The female makes a grass-lined nest in a chamber in the burrow and lays one to three rubbery eggs. Like a bird, she incubates the eggs by coiling her body around them. In about two weeks the eggs hatch into inch-long (2.5-cm) young that nurse by lapping milk secreted from glands into the fur on the mother's belly. The female does not have teats. The platypus is covered with soft, dense, molelike fur, and the male has a sharp venomous spine on each hind leg. Other local names for this unusual mammal are water mole and duck mole. A monotreme, its only close relative is the echidna, or spiny anteater (which see).

When the platypus was first brought to the attention of scientists in 1797, it was believed to be a hoax. Even when enough actual animals were produced to provide convincing evidence that it was real, the scientists did not know whether to classify it as a mammal or as some intermediate, perhaps even a reptile. Almost a century passed before its classification along with the echidnas was established.

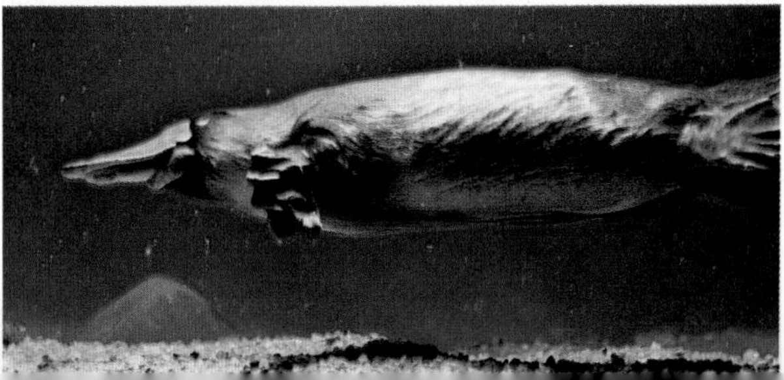

Proboscis Monkey

The male proboscis monkey *(Nasalis larvatus)* of Borneo ranks as the most grotesque of all monkeys because of its long, flabby, pouchlike nose. (Females have a short, snub nose.) This proboscis hangs about four inches over the mouth, and in old males it may be even longer—to six or seven inches (15.2–17.8 cm). When the monkey vocalizes, this bladderlike appendage inflates and stands up.

Tarsier

The tarsier *(Tarsius syrichta),* which inhabits the jungles of Borneo, Sumatra, and the Philippines, has tremendously large eyes in comparison to the size of the animal's body. If humans had eyes proportionately as large, for example, they would measure more than a foot across. The tarsier's body is no more than six inches long (15.2 cm), its tail almost a foot long (30.5 cm). Its head and ears are rounded, and its slender fingers and toes end in expanded adhesive pads used for clinging to the trunks and branches of trees. These primitive primates hop along the ground like frogs and may cover five or six feet

▲ Male proboscis monkey ▲ Tarsier

(1.5–1.8 m) with a single leap. They are normally active at night. During the day the pupils of their eyes are no larger than pinholes. Tarsiers are insect eaters.

Tuatara *(pronounced Too-a-tah-ra)*
Also called sphenodon, hatteria, or beakhead, the tuatara *(Sphenodon punctatus)* is the only living member of a group of reptiles that was abundant and widespread about 190 million years ago. These "living fossils" have a third eye in the middle of their head, just slightly behind their eyes. Covered by a transparent scale, the third eye is directly connected to a portion of the brain. In young tuataras, this eye is apparently capable of distinguishing light from dark; in adults, the "third eye" is generally overgrown with skin.

The sluggish, lizardlike tuatara is found only on islands off New Zealand and is now legally protected. About two feet long (61 cm), it has a row of spines from its neck down the middle of its back and tail. On the tail, the spines are saw-toothed like those on a snapping turtle. The tuatara lives in burrows that it digs itself or that it shares with the muttonbird, a petrel. Its diet consists mainly of insects, but it will also eat other small animals.

▲ Tuatara

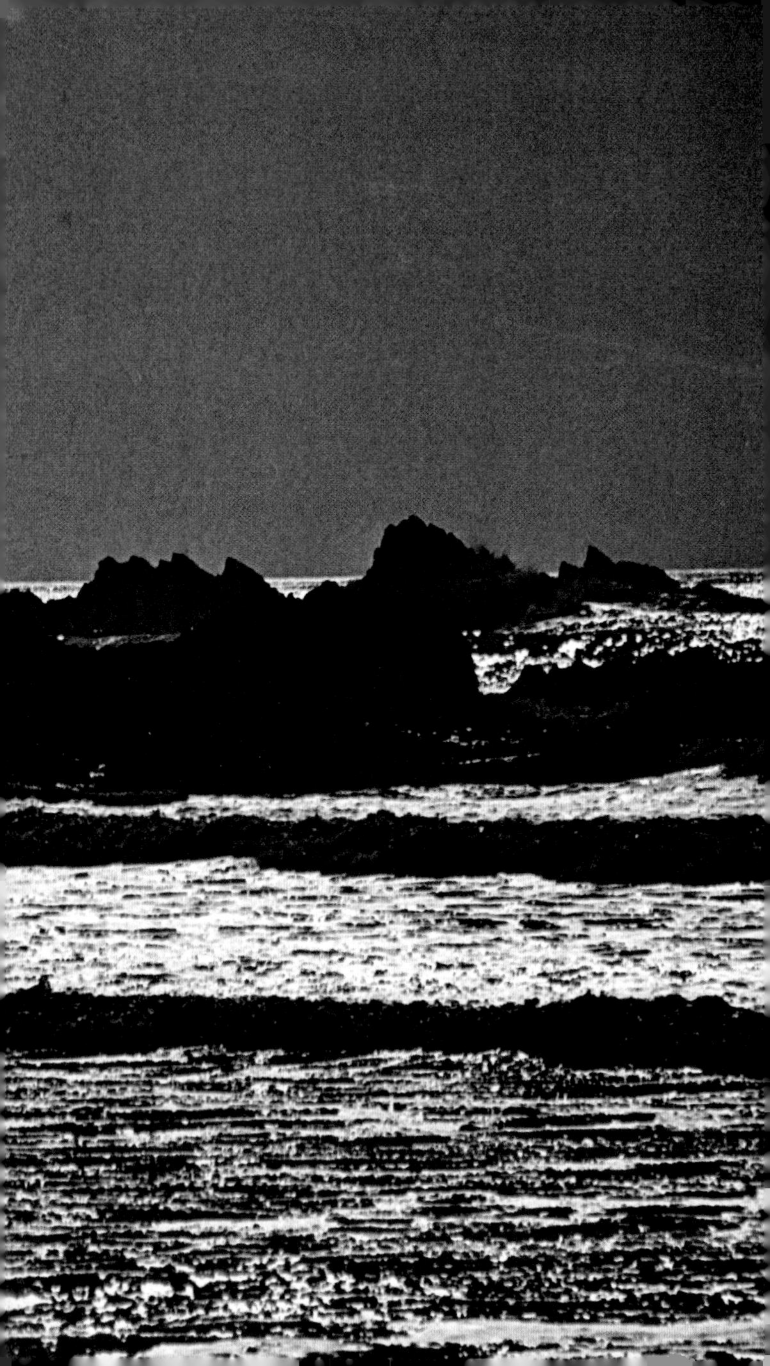

8

Seas

Albatross

Albatrosses *(Diomedea sp.)* are the most skilled of all birds in riding air currents, soaring and gliding so effortlessly that they seldom flap their wings. Their long, pointed wings are really not effective for normal flying, and on windless days albatrosses are almost helpless. Thirteen species of albatrosses roam the seas of the world, most abundant where the winds blow constantly.

Albatrosses nest in colonies on shore, some making a crude nest and others no nest at all. Before mating, males perform for the females, but their dances appear comical because of the birds' discomfort ashore. To launch themselves from land, albatrosses either run for a long distance or climb onto some sort of elevation, however slight. At sea, they run across the water's surface and then become airborne over a trough. Albatrosses stay on the wing at sea for months without landing, skimming the surface to drink and to pick up food. The wandering albatross *(Diomedea exulans),* largest of the clan, has a wingspread exceeding ten feet (3 m).

Blue Whale

The blue whale *(Balaenoptera musculus)* is the largest animal that has ever lived on land or in the sea, measuring to as much as a hundred feet long (30.5 m) and weighing to 125 tons

◀ Atlantic coast, Cornwall, England

(113,400 kg). Yet these giants sustain themselves on a diet of krill, straining these shrimp-sized crustaceans from the sea through the sheets of baleen, or whalebone, in their mouth. To stuff its stomach, a blue whale may sieve a ton of krill from the water.

This giant whale can dive to fifteen hundred feet (457.2 m) and remain submerged for more than two hours. Its capacious lungs may weigh as much as a ton, its heart more than half a ton. When it surfaces, a blue whale may "blow" or exhale for as long as five minutes to clear its lungs for a fresh supply of air.

A newborn whale may exceed twenty-five feet in length (7.6 m) and weigh as much as eight tons (7,258 kg).

Boxfish

An armored case completely encloses these fish of the family Ostraciidae, and they can swim only by using their pectoral fins and tail. Because of the hornlike projections over their eyes, they are sometimes called cowfish. Their dried bodies are often sold as curios. Boxfish are found in warm seas around the world.

Coelacanth *(pronounced See-la-canth)*

This "living fossil" *(Latimeria chalumnae)* represents a group of fishes believed extinct for about 300 million years until the late 1930s, when one was hauled in by commercial fishermen off the Comoro Islands between Africa and Madagascar. Several others have been netted in the same area since then, all taken in water from 250 to more than a thousand feet deep (76.2–304.8 m). The bottom-dwelling coelacanth has a big mouth and an oily, bulky body. The largest caught was about four feet long (1.2 m) and weighed 160 pounds (72.6 kg). The coelacanth's second dorsal, pelvic, and pectoral fins are at the ends of fleshy lobes, like those of its ancestors known only from fossil imprints.

Elephant Seal

Bull elephant seals *(Mirounga angustirostris)* weigh as much as three tons (2,721.6 kg) and may measure twenty-two feet in length (6.7 m); the females are about half as large. The bulls are distinctive because of their saclike snout, or proboscis, which may measure two feet long (61 cm) and stand almost vertical when distended with air. With this pouch acting as a resonator, the bull can make a wide range of bellows and snorts that announce his command over a territory and his harem. His harem usually consists of a dozen or so cows but may contain as many as fifty.

Elephant seals were once heavily harvested commercially, mainly for their blubber. Along the California coast they were reduced in numbers almost to extinction but are now making a comeback. The similar southern elephant seal *(Mirounga leonina),* also endangered, lives on islands off Antarctica.

▲ Albatross ▼Boxfish ▲ Northern elephant seal

Eulachon *(pronounced You-la-kon)*

An oily twelve-inch (30.5-cm) smelt living in the Pacific off northern North America, the eulachon *(Thaleichthys pacificus)* also goes by the name of candlefish locally. The Indians and some early white settlers dried the fish, inserted wicks in the bodies, and burned them for lights.

Flamingo

In any list of beautiful birds, the white, pink, or even scarlet flamingo rates somewhere near the top. The greater flamingo *(Phoenicopterus ruber),* which is widespread in the Caribbean, South America, Europe, Asia, and Africa, may stand

Flamingos ▲ Flounder camouflaged on sand ▶

almost five feet tall (1.5 m), both its neck and legs long and slim. In flight, a flamingo holds its neck straight out in front and its legs straight out behind. The flamingo's most unusual feature, however, is its peculiarly bent bill. When feeding, a flamingo turns its head upside-down and rakes its bill back and forth through the mud like a scoop. Both its fleshy tongue and its upper bill have serrated margins, and by pumping its tongue upward against the roof of its mouth, it forces water out of the bill, keeping only the mud enriched with organic matter inside.

Flamingos nest on mud flats, a mated pair building a circular mound of mud to as much as eighteen inches high (45.7 cm) and as wide or wider at the base. A shallow depression is left in the top for the egg. Exposed to the sun, this chimneylike structure soon dries hard. The female lays a single egg (rarely two), and then she and her mate take turns incubating it, sitting on the nest with their legs folded and sticking out to the rear.

Flounder

Flounders begin life looking like any other small fish, but in only a few days they begin to lean to one side—some species to the right, others to the left. The eye on the side toward which the fish is leaning begins to move upward, traveling almost all the way across the head so that both eyes are on top when the fish lies on its side. In nearly all species, the mouth twists upward, too. The transformation is completed within only a few weeks, the blind side of the flounder becoming white or cream-colored, since its pigments do not develop. Roughly five hundred species form the flatfish group, which includes some of the most valued and flavorful of all food fishes.

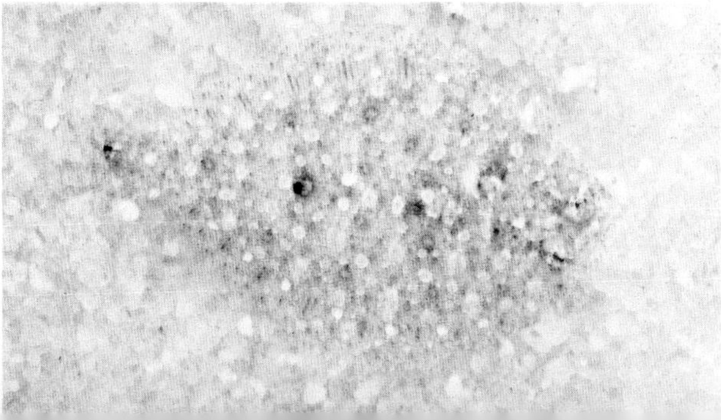

Flying Fish

Flying fishes *(Cypselurus sp., Parexocoetus sp., Exocoetus sp., Oxyporhamphus sp.,* and others*)* are common in warm seas throughout the world. Their "wings" are their enlarged and spineless pectoral fins, and in some species the pelvic fins also form gliding surfaces. A flying fish does not truly fly; it is strictly a glider. Swimming at a rapid speed, estimated by some to be forty miles per hour (64.4 km/hr), a flying fish explodes from the surface of the sea, then immediately stretches its "wings" and begins gliding. Usually it skims just above the surface, but in riding over the troughs of waves in high seas, it may at times be ten feet or more above the sea. As it loses speed, the fish drops downward tail-first, and as soon as its tail is in the water, it vibrates it rapidly. This sometimes gives the fish enough momentum to remain airborne for a bit longer. Typically, flying fishes stay in the air less than a minute at a time. In favorable winds, they may stay aloft longer and have been reported to glide for a quarter of a mile (402.3 m).

Frigate Bird

The frigate bird *(Fregata sp.)* has the largest wingspread (seven feet/2 m) in proportion to total body weight (about three and a half pounds/1.6 kg) of any bird. It is indeed a marvelous flying machine, and it can dive from several hundred feet in the air with deadly accuracy to pick up a small fish swimming near the surface without getting a feather wet. A frigate bird can also plummet from high in the sky to pluck a fish from another bird's bill or talons. These flight masters seem confidently aware of their ability to outfly any other bird in the sky. Another name for these magnificent feathered pirates is man-o'-war birds.

Frigate birds have webbed feet and can swim, but they seldom enter the water. On land they move clumsily, and like the albatrosses they need a strong wind and an open space for a long run to get airborne. The male magnificent frigate bird *(Fregata magnificens)* has an orange-red throat that becomes almost scarlet during the breeding season and is inflated to balloon size while he sits at the nest site waiting for the female to bring more sticks to complete the building. Four species of frigate birds roam the tropical and subtropical seas of the world.

◀ Flying fish ▲ Male frigate bird on nest

Goosefish

A giant among fish that "angle" for their food, the goosefish *(Lophius americanus)* reaches a length of four feet (1.2 m) and may weigh seventy pounds (31.8 kg). It ranges the full length of the Atlantic coast, coming into the shallows where the water is cool, retreating to deeper water where it is warm. The goosefish has a greatly flattened body and broad, armlike pectoral fins. The dorsal fins are reduced to thin, spiny filaments, the first with a flap of flesh at its tip. This hangs over the mouth like a lure, attracting small fish. The goosefish's mouth is enormous—so big, in fact, that it can swallow fish as large as itself. Inside the mouth are numerous sharp, back-curved teeth that keep prey from slipping out. When prey comes close, the goosefish simply opens this trap and allows the current to carry in its meal. The fish's name comes from its occasional catching of ducks or geese. Despite their ugliness, goosefish are good to eat, especially when caught in deep, cold water. Those inhabiting warmer, shallower water are softer and not as flavorful.

Many deep-sea fish "angle" for their food as the goosefish does. Often the lures at the tips of their modified fin filaments are luminous.

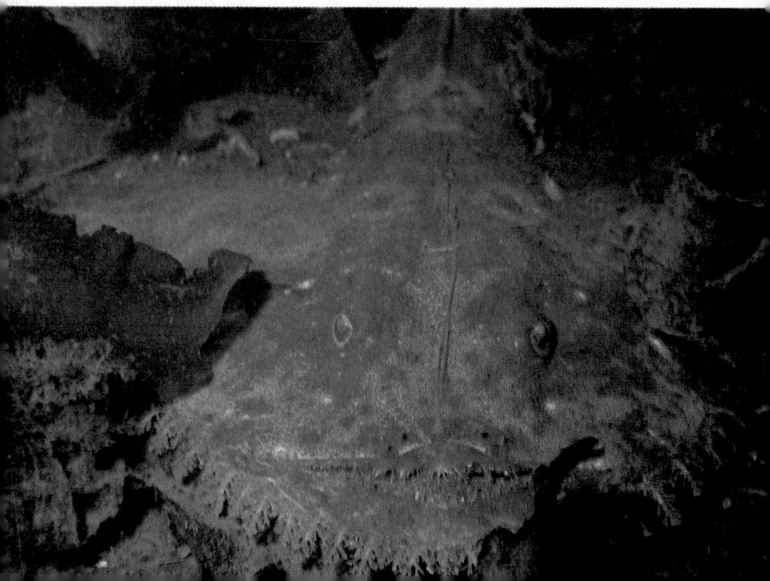

Grunion

The most extraordinary of all the spawning runs made by fish are those of the eight-inch (20.3-cm) California grunion *(Leuresthes tenuis),* which lives in the coastal waters off southern California. Every two weeks from March through June, and sometimes later, the grunion ride in on the peak waves of the highest tides of the full moon, millions of the silvery little fish swarming over the beaches. Quickly the females make pockets in the sand at the edge of the tide, and in these depressions they relieve their swollen abdomens of their load of eggs. The males, nearly wrapped around the females during this process, fertilize the eggs immediately, and as the next wave breaks over the beach, the fish are ready to be swept back into the sea, disappearing into its blackness. In less than a minute the spawning has been completed.

In the warm, moist sand the eggs are incubated, but they do not hatch until the next high tide bathes the sand where they were laid. Then the tiny hatchlings squirm up through the sand and wriggle into the water to be carried out to sea with the receding tide.

Gulper

Gulpers and swallowers are deep-sea fishes, found at depths of a mile or more (1,609.3 m) below the surface. One of the common gulpers *(Eurypharynx pelecanoides)* reaches a length of two feet (61 cm), but more than half of this length is its whiplike tail, which has a reddish luminous tip and is presum-

◀ Goosefish ▲ Grunion spawning

ably used as a lure. The gulper's mouth is astonishingly large, the lower jaw loosely hinged to the upper. This enables the gulper to take in prey even larger than itself.

Swallowers are similar to gulpers, one species *(Saccopharynx ampullacrus)* attaining a length of six feet (1.8 m). It also has an exceptionally long tail with a lighted tip, and it is believed to wrap this tail around its prey in a snakelike fashion to help hold it until it can be swallowed. Like many fishes of the deep sea where food is not plentiful, a swallower cannot afford to miss an opportunity for a meal. Its stomach can be stretched to accommodate a fish several times larger than the swallower's normal size.

Hagfish

Ugly and repulsive are apt words for the slimy-bodied hagfishes *(Myxine sp.* and *Eptatretus sp.),* the most primitive of all living fishes. A hagfish lacks fins and jaws, and its eyes are grown over with skin, the fish presumably able to distinguish only light from dark. A hagfish feeds on dead or injured fish, frequently attacking those caught in the nets of commercial fishermen. With its toothy tongue, the hagfish rasps a hole in its victim and then continues to eat its way inside, consuming all but the skin and bones.

All hagfishes wear a rosette of sensory tentacles on their snout. They are worldwide in distribution in cold, deep waters and occur from the continental shelf to depths of four thousand feet (1,219 m). None is longer than two and a half feet (76.2 cm); most species are shorter.

Hagfish ▲ King salmon ▶

King Salmon

King or chinook salmon *(Oncorhynchus tshawytscha)* are the largest of all the salmons. Though they average ten pounds or less (4.5 kg), one weighing 126½ pounds (57.4 kg) was netted by commercial fishermen, and an 83-pounder (37.6 kg) was caught on rod and reel.

King salmon make the longest spawning run of any fish. Those living in the Bering Sea off the coast of Alaska travel up the Yukon River to Lake Teslin in Canada, a trip of more than 2,400 miles (3,861.6 km), and a climb to an altitude of 2,200 feet (670.6 m). The journey takes about two months, during which time the salmon continually swim upstream at a rate of forty miles per day (64.4 km).

During their upstream trip, the males change drastically in appearance, their jaws becoming elongated and so grotesquely hooked they can no longer close. The teeth also grow slim and daggerlike. Both the females and the males are emaciated from the lack of food on their trip, their fins frayed and their eyes sunken in their sockets. When they reach the spawning area, the females immediately make a nest, or redd, in the gravel and lay their eggs there. Simultaneously the males spread their milt over the gravelly beds, fertilizing the eggs.

Exhausted, their task of procreation accomplished, the salmon struggle out of the shallow water at the spawning site and are swept downstream by the current. Soon they die. The eggs hatch in about two months, some of the young moving seaward immediately, others spending at least a year in the stream before going out to sea. At sea they may live for two to eight years before getting the spawning urge that sends them back to the same stream where they were hatched. They are apparently guided there by an odor imprint.

All of the Pacific salmon have similar spawning habits. Atlantic salmon *(Salmo salar)* also spawn in the headwaters of streams, but most adults make a successful return trip to the sea and may spawn several times in their lifetime.

Lantern-Eye Fish

These unusual fish *(Anomalops katoptron)* have "headlights" which they can turn on or off at will. Under each eye is another eyelike structure with a transparent covering in which colonies of luminous bacteria live. The bacteria produce light continuously, but the fish can either expose them or keep them concealed.

Some species in this family (Anomalopidae) have a fold of skin that can be drawn over the lights to turn them off. In others the whole light organ can be rotated downward to turn it off, up to turn it on. Most lantern-eye fish are small, measuring only about three inches in length (7.6 cm), but some that live in the Indo-Pacific region are as much as a foot long (30.5 cm). The Indo-Pacific and the Caribbean are the only seas inhabited by lantern-eye fish.

Leatherback Turtle

Marine leatherbacks *(Dermochelys coriacea)* are the behemoths of the turtle world and the largest of all living reptiles, reaching a length of nine feet (2.7 m) and weighing to fifteen hundred pounds (680.4 kg). They average five to six feet long (1.5–1.8 m) and weigh about a thousand pounds (453.6 kg). Like other marine turtles, these giants have limbs that are modified into flippers for swimming. A leatherback's front flippers are so streamlined they look almost like a swallow's

Manatee ▶

wings, and in a six-foot turtle they may span nine feet. With these "wings" the leatherback swims with ease and speed, roaming the open seas of the tropics. Like other sea turtles, however, the leatherback must come to shore to lay its eggs, the female laboriously dragging her gargantuan body over the beach to just above the high-tide line. There she digs a hole with her hind flippers and lays her eggs, then immediately heads back to sea. The eggs are left in the carefully covered hole to be incubated by the heat of the sun. When they hatch, the young must dig themselves out and make their way to the sea on their own.

Unlike any other turtles, the leatherback does not have a horny shell. The bony plates forming its carapace are covered with a thick, leathery skin, and seven distinct ridges extend down the turtle's back.

Manatee

Unbelievable as it may seem, these gentle but very ugly beasts are said to have spawned the mermaid myth. In days gone by, both manatees *(Trichetus sp.)* and closely related dugongs *(Dugong dugon)* were much more abundantly distributed in

seas around the world. Today the few remaining animals are confined to coastal areas of subtropical and tropical seas.

The Florida manatee or sea cow *(Trichetus manatus)* is one of these endangered species, its population reduced to a critical low. Overkilling is partly responsible, for like manatees everywhere, they were once prized as food. Steller's sea cow *(Hydrodamalis stelleri),* for example, was a giant of the clan living on islands in the Bering Sea, but it was harvested so heavily that it was annihilated in less than half a century after its discovery. All manatees have a low reproductive rate, the females typically producing only one calf every other year. Another factor contributing to the decline of manatees has been the destruction of their habitat as coastal areas have been settled. In Florida, many manatees have become victims of the whirling propellers of outboards.

But mermaids? Only a sailor who had been at sea for many months or who had visited one too many bars in port could possibly see beauty in these beasts. Bulkily fishlike in general body shape and weighing as much as a ton (907.2 kg), a manatee has thick, almost totally hairless skin and is usually encrusted with barnacles if it has been living in salt water, or slimed with green algae if it has been living in fresh water. Its front legs are heavy flippers, it has no hind legs, and its tail is either rounded or flattened horizontally into flukes for swimming. Its head is broad, its eyes are small, and it has no external ears. Its muzzle is broad and bristly. Manatees do not have front teeth, and their lips are divided into two highly mobile halves that are used for grasping.

Manta

Like the whale shark and the basking shark, the mantas *(Manta sp.* and *Mobula sp.)* are giants of their clan—the rays. An Atlantic manta *(Manta birostris)* measures as much as twenty feet across its extended "wings," or pectoral fins, and it may weigh one and a half tons (1,360.8 kg). Sometimes called devilfish, the big manta is actually harmless, causing injuries only when trying to escape from a hook, harpoon, or trap. The formidable-looking "horns" on each side of its head are actually fleshy fins used for channeling food into its mouth.

Mola

Also called ocean sunfish, the mola *(Mola mola)* is one of the giants of the sea, reaching a length of ten feet and weighing six hundred pounds or more (272.2 kg). This big fish also goes by the name headfish because it does appear to be all head. Its mouth is very small and has a bony beak. The mola has large dorsal and anal fins directly opposed at the rear of the body, and it has a narrow, fringelike caudal fin but no caudal peduncle, or constriction between the body and the tail. In the open sea, the mola typically floats on its side. It is not a strong swimmer, and currents may carry it into cool water, where it is helpless. The mola belongs to the same order of fishes (Tetraodontiformes) as puffers and triggerfish (which see).

Mudskipper

The mudskipper *(Periophthalmus barbarus)* is a four- to five-inch (10.2–12.7-cm) froglike goby that lives on the mud flats along mangrove shores of the Indo-Pacific region. When the tide moves out, the mudskippers stay on the flats. They have long pectoral fins with which they propel themselves, hopping about like frogs. Their big, bulging eyes also contribute to their froglike appearance. Mudskippers do not have to go back into the water as long as their gills are kept moist.

▲ Manta

Narwhal *(pronounced Nar-wil)*
The narwhal *(Monodon monoceros)* is the unicorn of the whale clan, for the males have a single greatly enlarged incisor tooth or tusk, usually the left one. Straight in some but most often twisted or spiraled, this big tooth may be as much as eight feet long (2.4 m)—more than 50 percent longer than the whale's body. The tusk projects straight forward like a spear. Rarely, tusks develop on both sides, each spiraled in the same direction, and occasionally a female develops a tusk. The function of this oversized tooth remains a mystery. It may be used in probing for food, though this is doubtful, or it may be only a secondary sexual characteristic, like a man's beard. The narwhal occurs circumpolarly in the Arctic.

Oarfish
The odd oarfish *(Regalecus glesne)* has a flat, ribbonlike body, almost transparent, bluish, and to as much as twenty feet long (6 m). Its pectoral fins are thin red filaments, and its red dorsal fin extends from head to tail, forming a plumed, crownlike crest on the head. When washed ashore, its fragile body dries and deteriorates rapidly. This strange fish is believed responsible for at least some of the sea serpent tales.

▲ Mudskippers

The closely related ribbonfish *(Trachipterus iris)* also has an extremely thin body. A six-foot (1.8-m) ribbonfish inhabiting the Pacific off northern North America was called king-of-the-salmon by the Indians, who believed it controlled the appearance and abundance of salmon.

The oarfish lives near the surface, roaming the seas of the world. Most ribbonfish are found in deep water.

Pelican

A brown pelican's beak may be as much as twelve inches long (30.5 cm), and the pouch beneath it can hold three gallons or more (11.4 l) of water when distended. The brown pelican *(Pelecanus occidentalis)* does not store food in its pouch, but it does use the pouch to help it catch fish. Soaring above the sea—pelicans become airborne laboriously, but they fly, soar, and glide with ease and grace—a pelican suddenly turns beak-downward and plunges into the water, sometimes diving from a height of fifty feet or more (15.2 m) and hitting the water with a great splash, but seldom going completely under. Or a pelican bobbing about on the surface may upend in the water. Though it is not infallible, a pelican nearly always makes its catch.

▲ Brown pelican

A pelican would never win a beauty contest, for it is one of the most grotesque of all birds. It has tremendous webbed feet, short legs, a hunchbacked posture, and a flabby pouch. But it is superbly designed for its role as a fish catcher. Six species occur in temperate to warm regions throughout the world. The brown pelican, now an endangered species, inhabits mainly coastal regions but sometimes ranges inland. It has a wingspread of about six feet (1.8 m). The American white pelican's *(Pelecanus erythrorhynchos)* wingspread is nine feet or more (2.7 m), and it has the unusual habit of hunting cooperatively, a flock working together to chase a school of fish into the shallows where all the birds then share in the harvest. The Dalmatian pelican *(Pelecanus philippensis),* widely distributed in Asia, wears a fringe of curly feathers on its neck.

Puffer

Some puffers *(Sphoeroides sp., Lagocephalus sp., Canthigaster sp.,* and others*)* gulp air, others water, and still others take in both air and water—but however they do it, the result is the same: a greatly inflated body. Once inflated, the fish turns belly-up at the surface. The sudden and dramatic increase in size either scares or discourages most attackers. When the danger has passed, the puffer deflates by belching out the air or water, quickly returning to its normal size.

 A puffer's teeth are fused to form two teeth above and two

▲ Puffer

below. This beak is used to crush the shells of crabs or other crustaceans. A puffer can also make loud noises by grinding its teeth. Puffers live in warm seas throughout the world. The smooth puffer *(Lagocephalus laevigatus)* attains a length of two feet (61 cm) and may weigh seven pounds (3.2 kg), but most are less than half that size.

Remora

The remora or sharksucker *(Remora remora)* is a hitchhiking scavenger. Its dorsal fin has been modified into a powerful sucking disc consisting of a series of ridges and spaces that create a vacuum for attachment to a host. As the remora slides backward, the suction increases; if it swims forward, the suction lessens until the remora finally releases itself. A remora attaches to a shark or some other fish and then rides effortlessly wherever the larger fish goes. When its host finds food, the remora detaches and feeds on the scraps.

Remoras and related suckerfishes are found in warm seas around the world. The largest is the sharksucker *(Echeneis naucrates)*, which measures three feet long (91.4 cm); most are smaller. Natives of the Caribbean used to tie a line to a remora's tail and then turn it loose when a big turtle was sighted basking at the surface. The remora would head immediately for the turtle, and as soon as it fastened itself, the catch could be hauled back to the boat.

▲ Sharksuckers (remoras)

Sea Catfish

Male sea catfish *(Arius sp.* and *Bagre sp.)* are among nature's most dutiful parents—up to a point. As the female lays her eggs, the male picks them up and holds them in his mouth until they hatch, sometimes becoming the custodian of three or four dozen pea-sized eggs. After the eggs hatch, the young continue to use his mouth as a place of refuge. During this entire time, the male does not eat, nature having wisely curbed his appetite. But the day finally comes when the male is ravenously hungry and ready to eat his fill of whatever is near and available. Then he will devour his own offspring if they are not quick to recognize that their days of being coddled are now in the past.

Seahorse

Seahorses *(Hippocampus sp.)* are so unusual in appearance and habits that they are scarcely recognizable as fish. Their head is bent at a right angle to the body, and the mouth is extended into a slim snout with which they can probe deeply into crevices for morsels of food. Their body is encased in an armor of bony rings (they have no scales), and the tail is prehensile, used for holding onto seaweed. A seahorse swims gracefully, moving its body vertically through the water. It is propelled by the rapid vibration of the dorsal fin. A seahorse has an extraordinarily large air bladder with which it can regulate the level at which it swims.

A female seahorse lays her eggs in the brood pouch on a male's belly. He fertilizes the eggs immediately, and carries them with him until they hatch. Newly hatched seahorses are tiny replicas of the adults, and they continue to use their father's pouch as a place of refuge.

Pipefishes *(Sygnathus sp.)* belong to the same family as seahorses and live in the same habitat. They have a long, slim body, an eight-inch (20.3-cm) pipefish no bigger around than a pencil. Like seahorses, they have a tubular snout, and the body is encased in horny rings. But pipefishes swim horizontally. Male pipefish have a pouch and brood the eggs and young just as seahorses do.

 Sea moths *(Pegasus sp.)* are similar in body structure to

seahorses but are not closely related to them. Their mouth is at the tip of a mothlike proboscis, and their enlarged pectoral fins stick out at the sides like moth wings. Sea moths are found only in the Indo-Pacific region.

Sea Lamprey

Jawless and nearly as ugly as the closely related hagfish (which see), the sea lamprey *(Petromyzon marinus)* lives in the North Atlantic, moving into freshwater lakes and streams to spawn. Those that became landlocked in the Great Lakes, gaining entry through the Welland Canal that permitted them to bypass Niagara Falls, proliferated and eventually destroyed the fish that supported a commercial fishing industry in the lakes.

▲ "Pregnant" male seahorse

Biologists finally developed a selected-kill chemical that eliminates the lampreys at their spawning areas, allowing a slow build-up of commercial fishing again.

A sea lamprey, which may reach a length of three feet (91.4 cm), is a parasite. With its round suckerlike mouth filled with circular rows of teeth, the lamprey attaches to the side of its prey and tears a hole through which the victim's blood and body fluids are sucked. Anticoagulants from glands in the lamprey's mouth keep the blood flowing in the wound. When the prey no longer yields enough blood to be satisfying and is dead or nearly so, the lamprey detaches itself and searches out another victim.

Unlike the hagfish, the lamprey has well-developed eyes. It also has dorsal and caudal fins but no paired fins. Included in the parasitic sea lamprey's family (there is a parasitic species in the Pacific as well as in the Atlantic) are more than half a dozen nonparasitic lampreys that live in fresh water, most of them less than ten inches long (25.4 cm).

Soapfish

If it is handled, or even if there is a commotion nearby, a soapfish *(Rypticus sp.)* surrounds itself with a frothy, soaplike mucus. This secretion is irritating and may be poisonous to an intruder. The soapfish is widely distributed in the Atlantic.

Slipmouths *(Leiognathus sp.)*, members of a different family inhabiting the Indo-Pacific, also give off a soapy mucus. They have a tubelike mouth that is extended when they are feeding but withdrawn at other times.

Swordfish

A giant swordfish *(Xiphias gladius)* may be fifteen feet long (4.6 m) and weigh more than half a ton (453.6 kg). A quarter of its length is accounted for by its flat, sharp bill. The swordfish has no scales or teeth. When feeding, it charges through a school of fish by slashing its bill from side to side, then returns to pick up any of the fish that have been stunned. This big fish roams the warm seas of the world.

Marlins, or billfishes, also have a bill, but it is round and shorter than the swordfish's. A blue marlin *(Makaira nigricans)* may weigh up to fifteen hundred pounds (680.4 kg).

Triggerfish

Triggerfish *(Balistes sp., Canthidermis sp., Balistapus sp.,* and others*)* are so called because the third spine of their dorsal fin serves as a trigger, allowing the second dorsal spine to be slid either forward or backward. In its forward position, it holds the high first spine of the dorsal fin firmly in place. The triggerfish lifts its first dorsal spine to anchor itself in crevices in coral or other rocks. Several dozen species of triggerfishes are found in warm waters around the world. All have a leathery, slimeless skin.

In filefish *(Aluterus sp., Monacanthus sp., Oxymonacanthus sp.,* and others*)*, closely related to triggerfish, the dorsal fin has been reduced to a single spine that in many species is saw-toothed at the rear.

◀ Soapfish ▲ Triggerfish

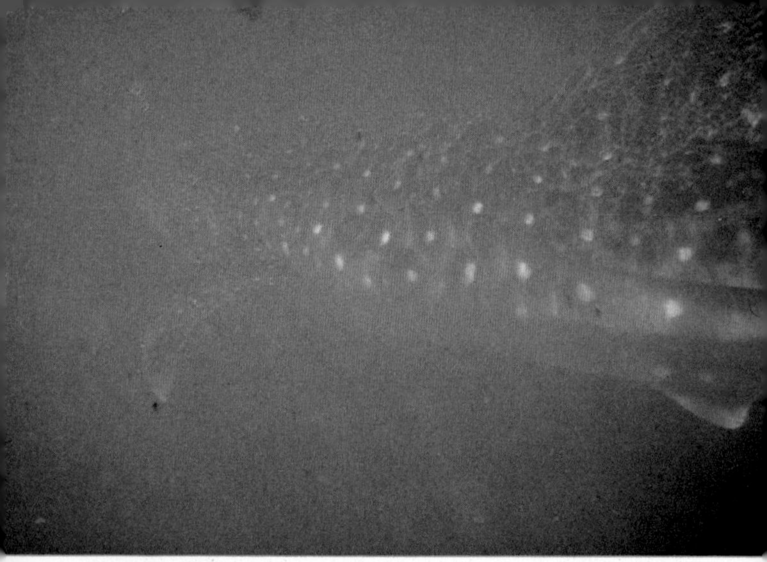

Viperfish

One of the most commonly illustrated of all the deep-sea fish, these awesome monsters *(Chauliodus sp.)* are fortunately no larger than twelve inches (30.5 cm). Their mouth is studded with extremely long needle-sharp teeth. If prey is not impaled when the fish closes it mouth, it is nevertheless trapped in the toothy cage of the enormous mouth. When a viperfish closes its mouth, its spikelike teeth overlap the jaws.

Whale Shark

The giant among sharks and the largest fish in the sea is the whale shark *(Rhincolon typus),* averaging about twenty-five feet (7.6 m) but known to reach a length of fifty feet (15.2 m). The estimated weight for one of these behemoths is fifteen tons (13,608 kg). Despite its imposing size, this giant is docile. Swimmers and divers have not only probed them but also climbed aboard to examine the monsters more closely. The whale shark, which roams seas throughout the world, feeds on plankton that it collects on the mesh of its gill rakers.

Another giant in the clan is the basking shark *(Cetorhinus maximus),* known to reach a length of forty feet (12.2 m). It also makes its meals of plankton. The basking shark is a member of a different family, however, and lives in cool seas.

▲ Whale shark

Index *Picture references in italics*

George Kensinger became interested in strange creatures when, as a boy, he watched newborn opossums, no bigger than honeybees, crawling along a slime track to their mother's pouch. In the years since then, Kensinger has discovered many other animals that are in some manner equally unusual. This book is a result of that pursuit, with the author's training as a biologist giving meaning to his observations and interpretations.